Worming and Spinning for Trout

Worming

and Spinning for Trout

By Jerome B. Wood

A. S. BARNES AND COMPANY • NEW YORK

Printed in the United States of America

Foreword

FIFTY YEARS AGO, BEFORE OUR NATURAL RESOURCES WERE damaged by improvements and the automobile changed the face of the land, it was no great trick to go out and "catch a mess of trout." As a boy, this old addict could mount his bicycle and within twenty minutes float a worm in any one of five different trout streams, all good, and return with a sizable catch in ample time to grease the skillet with a fat slab of salt pork before the hungry farm-hands trooped in from the fields.

Slowly but surely, the trout became scarcer and wiser. Anglers began to pay attention to such things as wind, temperatures and water. Barometers were consulted. Eventually came the day when the reward was not worth the effort and the bamboo whip was retired to the attic. It seemed like the end of a fond dream.

Then along came Jerry Wood. There are perfectionists in all fields, but they are few and our skepticism was aroused. However, his contagious enthusiasm and a driving desire to excel were a bit intriguing and we finally dusted off the rod and creel, patched up the boots and went along to see what it was all about.

To our amazement we caught trout. Furthermore, we discovered we knew little or nothing about trout fishing, despite a half-century of exposure to the art and the memory of many a well-stuffed creel. We confirmed a suspicion that a high degree of technical skill is required to catch trout under modern conditions.

How did Jerry Wood acquire that skill? One way was by placing a chair on the front lawn and practice-casting by the hour, the object being to place the lure neatly under the bottom rung. Perhaps this business is for fanatics only.

At any rate, here is an unconditional guarantee: the angler who follows the methods outlined in this book will catch trout. However, there is one all-important requisite. He must acquire the skill to make the techniques effective. He must practice, practice, PRACTICE. When he can thread a No. 14 hook on a two-pound-test line, deftly attach a strip of matchbook sinker, stand across the room from a quart fruit jar and drop the hook into the jar eight out of ten times with swinging casts, he is ready for the big day.

It may not be the ideal day for trouting. The author of this book is no crack-of-dawn fisherman and he does not pay too much attention to the weather. I have seen him amble up to a stream at high noon, with the water low and a hot sun overhead and emerge from the brush two hours later with four or five fat trout in the basket.

If the reader will adhere faithfully to the instructions contained herein and discipline himself to constant practice of the necessary techniques he will suddenly find that he is catching trout. Happy Snags!

RALPH E. SPINNING

Boston, New York

Contents

Illustrations

Introduction

"IF THERE IS ONE FACTOR MORE IMPORTANT THAN ANY other in catching brown trout consistently, I'd say it is the ability to recognize fully—and keep it in mind every second you are on a stream—the extreme wariness and delicate sensitivity of the fish you are trying to take.

"If they see you, you don't have much chance. If they hear you or feel your presence through ground vibrations, you're sunk again. If you don't fish your lure in a way that is almost identical with the way they see their natural food, all but small fish will turn away from it. No angler dares to underestimate a brown trout if he wants to put fish in the creel."

The foregoing reflective comment was made by one of the most intelligent men I've ever known. He made it while we were driving home from a day of fishing on a trout stream abounding with fish. He is a good angler but inclined to forget or ignore techniques he knows well. He hadn't started to take fish until I caught up with him on the stream about midday and, after watching a few minutes, pointed out some flaws he'd permitted to develop in his technique.

The comment is an excellent in-a-nutshell outline of the mandatory do's and don'ts for a good trout angler. You can be a fine caster, your tackle can be of the best, you may know where there are loads of trout; yet, unless you reckon fully with the wiliness of brown trout, you may come home empty-handed.

In the pages to follow, the emphasis is placed on the techniques that may be used to cope with the fears, the sensitivity, and natural appetites of this great game fish, as well as other less wary trout.

Worming and Spinning for Trout

chapter 1

The Art of Worming

ALEC HENDERSON IS A LEGEND ALONG WESTERN NEW YORK trout streams. Oldtimers, including some of the finest dry-fly purists in the country, still speak of his exploits with awe. Most of them speak with admiration, even though Alec always fished with a lowly earthworm. The admiration was mixed with envy. It was a rare day in which Alec wasn't high man in any group of trout anglers, both in number of fish and size of fish. His skill with a worm, his knowledge of trout water, his masterful approaches to trout hides were sheer artistry.

Alec never talked much. He was a typical Scotsman, sure of his ability to catch good trout under almost any condition, high water or low, cold water or warm. He passed out few tips to his companions but always gave them their choice of the water. Then, taking the second-best or third-best stretch, he'd invariably return with the most and best trout.

Many times I've seen him start up a heavily fished stream behind other anglers who were pounding the most likely

spots. When he'd overtake them, hours later, or they'd
check with him on their way back downstream, strangers
invariably would be amazed by the heavy creel of fish Alec
would be carrying. Quite a few of those with light or
empty creels also had been using worms.

Some secretly watched Alec practice his art and tried to
copy his technique but, at that time, no one even came
close. Alec was in a class by himself.

Alec had his little weaknesses, however. Even though
he said little, his bulging creels pleased his ego greatly. You
could see that by the proud gleam in his eye when he'd
return to the car. But, whether he needed the fish for himself or not, he'd always go for the limit. In those days the
limit was twenty fish. Alec usually had all the law would
allow. Most of the fish would be large. Often, the ten-
pound weight limit stopped him before he had twenty fish.
Unless he had hurt them, he'd seldom keep trout under ten
or twelve inches. Usually, he aimed for twelve inches and
larger. Some of us who saw, heard, and read about Alec's
fabulous catches felt more than envy. We acquired a strong
desire to emulate him in everything except the number of
fish killed.

A small group of anglers, including myself, decided that
much more skill and know-how was required to pursue
Alec's worming art than any type of fly-fishing. We decided to make a joint, determined effort to learn everything
about Alec's technique.

One of us would try to fish with him. He'd show or
demonstrate little when you were near but you could
sometimes sneak up behind a bush, sometimes watch with
field glasses. There was no secret about his tackle. That he
would show freely. It was as light and delicate as that we
used when casting with a No. 14 dry fly.

Our group gradually started forming some convictions
on worming techniques. In winter months, we'd hold bull

sessions at each other's homes and compare notes. We'd reason and we'd argue. We started to acquire worming equipment, to practice the precise placing of a worm, to develop ideas of our own. The latter was important to our ego. We couldn't copy Alec blindly. We had to consider tackle and methods we hoped might be superior in the same way an amateur fly-tier tries to develop a hot new pattern.

None of us succeeded in a hurry. It took years before we even came close to Alec and many more years before we acquired sufficient skill to feel that we were even remotely comparable. In the end, a few of us finally attained the satisfaction of catching trout when no one else was taking them, of taking larger fish on the average than most anyone we encountered. At least two of our gang now are discussed by other trout anglers with almost the same awe we used to have for Alec Henderson.

All of the gang, fortunately, are conservationists in the strict sense. Except for two or three good-sized fish, and the few fish we may unintentionally injure, we usually release our trout. At times, all of us have released fish as large as two and three pounds when we felt we had enough in our creel. Even on crowded streams, we often are able to take dozens of fish—releasing the majority of them—on days when other anglers are doing little.

There is a real danger in writing this book. If too many anglers became skilled in the art of worming and, at the same time, didn't practice conservation, the trout hatcheries couldn't keep stocked the heavily fished streams of the East. Then, even the worm artist would have nothing.

After an angler becomes sufficiently proficient to realize that he can catch trout just about any time he wants them, however, he feels less compelled to satisfy his ego. He finds that his ego is lifted even more by the satisfaction he gets from releasing fish of a size he knows many other anglers have never attained. Furthermore, here's a fish he may catch again.

But we can dismiss the dangers of excessive fish kills by skilled wormers because most anglers, despite what they may learn in this book, never will become artists with a worm any more than others, like myself, will ever become Rembrandts. No book can do more than teach. The worming comes with diligent practice and, above all, a keen ability to observe and apply the observations to conditions on that particular day. Most anglers just will not take the time to do a thorough job.

I've taken many friends under my wing and tried to teach them what I have learned in years of experiments and stream study. All of them caught more fish as a result of coaching but I'd guess that only one out of twenty will ever make a top worm angler.

Most anglers cannot or will not work or concentrate hard enough to solve all the problems, which are far more complex and interesting than those in any other type of fishing I know. However, many of those friends have expressed the wish they could have in writing all the points of the worming technique. Study them well. If you apply them artfully, you are virtually certain to catch trout every time you fish good water.

Let no one assume that I prefer worming to a fly. I still lean strongly to the dainty, if phony, feathers for all kinds of fish, from trout to Atlantic salmon, bonefish, snook, and steelheads.

There are many streams and many conditions, however, particularly in the East, where a properly-handled worm will give you far more action than any fly and great satisfaction in the knowledge that you are doing something that requires more skill and angling knowledge.

chapter 2

Worming Tackle

ALEC HENDERSON ALWAYS TRIED, WHENEVER POSSIBLE, TO use a short line. Obviously, he believed that the ideal way of handling a worm was to have the bait at all times almost directly under the tip of his extremely long rod.

Alec's line seldom was extended more than the length of his rod. With this short line, he could place a worm with uncanny accuracy. More important, he was able to avoid almost completely any unnatural drag on the worm. We surmised then—and later found it to be completely correct—that here was the key to the art of worming.

Ideally, the worm must drift naturally down the stream at the same speed it would move if it were unhampered by a sinker. There must be no sideward movement caused by current drag on the line. The worm must not move faster than the current in which it is drifting. It should not move much slower. The worm must be on the bottom, as it would be if it had just fallen into the water from a crumbling bank.

Try dropping a small worm into a shallow riffle and

observe its movements and its course. If the current isn't too fast, the squirming worm will catch frequently on the corners of rocks and pebbles and go downstream at a speed about one-half or one-third the speed of the current. If you can come close to duplicating that movement when you have line and sinker attached, you have mastered the basic technique. Add to that the knowledge of where trout lie and how to approach the suspected trout "hide." The remainder of your problem is acquiring stream knowledge, a knowledge you need for any type of trout angling.

It's as simple or as difficult as that, depending on your adaptability, your powers of observation, and your determination to learn. In between are many contributory steps.

I doubt if there are more ardent disciples of Alec Henderson than the Evans brothers and myself. We're all experimenters. Dave Evans and I are strong advocates of the long rod, as long a rod as you can handle without excessive arm strain. Dave has even gone into imported bamboo rods in lengths ranging to twelve feet in his efforts to stay away from wary trout and still use a short line. Powerful as it is, however, Dave's wrist cannot take such a long rod for any period of time. He's backed down on length. So have I.

My present favorite is ten feet long, weighing about seven ounces. I've never since acquired a rod, however, that equalled the seven-ounce, ten-and-a-half-foot rod which some person mysteriously was able to find secreted in grass along the East Branch of the Ausable River in the Adirondack Mountains one day while I was coaching a friend fishing a few hundred yards upstream. I'd still like to get a ten-and-a-half-foot glass job in that weight with sufficient backbone. I know I could have one made on special order, but I dislike paying a king's ransom for a rod that needs little more than moderate backbone.

Ivor Evans uses a shorter rod and does as well as we do by using a longer line and constantly mending it to avoid drag. There is no doubt that the longer rod makes the job easier. Ivor confessed to me only recently he's on the lookout for a long rod. For myself, I feel helpless with anything shorter than nine feet.

Any old reel that will hold a good length of monofilament line will do. In recent years, virtually all of our worming clique has swung over to monofilament, partly because it is easier to handle and partly because it permits some new techniques that even old Alec couldn't master without monofilament. There was no monofilament when Alec was king.

The smaller diameter of monofilament obviously makes the line less visible to the fish, but this is not too important in view of the fact that we use long leaders when we are handling a conventional fly line. The decisive factor is that there is far less water drag on monofilament to cause the worm to act unnaturally. The trouble with monofilament is that it is hard to see, and you must be able to watch its downstream course constantly so that you can follow it with your rod tip.

Terminal tackle is important. We often go down to 4X leader tips on clear, low streams. Even in discolored water, we seldom have tips heavier than four-pound test. On average water, most of us use two-pound test. With such light leaders, we lose many "lunkers." We lose much tackle. But if we don't lose much tackle, we know we are fishing improperly. The latter tenet must be accepted philosophically but without question for virtually all trout water.

I recall the bright, hot day in June when Irv Conrad and I were fishing a lovely stretch on the lower Wiscoy in Western New York. The stretch was filled with wonderful hides for trout—little log-and-brush jams, glassy runs under overhanging alders and viny growths over undercut banks. Irv worked upstream from our parking place. I walked downstream several hundred yards and started up behind him.

Irv is a fine wormer. He's one of the original members of the worming clique. But he's also a magnificent golfer and he divides his time between his two loves. On this day, Irv forgot one of the tenets. When I caught up with Irv several hours later, he looked a little glum. He had only a few fair-sized trout. I had three heavy browns and had released about a half-dozen other nice fish.

I approached Irv along the bank. He had not seen me. I watched him for a few minutes before I made my presence known. Irv is six feet, four inches tall and extremely graceful for a man that size. He uses his height and long reach to great advantage in floating his worm, leaning far ahead to reduce the length of line required to reach a hide. But on the particular pool he was fishing, I noticed that he was placing his worm nearly a foot short of the position in which it should have dropped. His worm never came sufficiently close to the pile of brush that had created the pool. I wondered why; Irv certainly knew better.

I called to him and he waded out of the stream. We sat on a log, lighted cigarettes, and compared notes.

"I've been fishing hard, Jerry, but they don't seem to be hitting," Irv complained. Then, a little proudly: "But I haven't lost a single tackle."

I suggested that maybe the reason he hadn't taken fish was because he hadn't lost tackle. His eyes lightened.

"Maybe you've got something there, pal. I think I'll try this pool again. It sure looks good to me." He studied the pool he had just been fishing. We finished our cigarettes and Irv waded out again. I sat and watched.

His first cast was only an inch or so from the brush
pile. For a moment, his worm did hook up on a projecting, underwater twig but then swept free. Irv's rod tip
followed the worm downstream smoothly. Then the line
stopped. There was that thrilling quiver of the monofilament and then it started to straighten out as the fish moved
back under the brush. Irv struck powerfully and the trout
was out in open water before it realized what was happening. It leaped, almost hooking the line on a projecting
branch, then raced upstream into a shallow riffle leading
into the pool. Then it slid downstream again toward the
brush pile and Irv skillfully backed up onto the dry bank
to apply sideway pressure. The trout leaped again, then
started to bore toward the hide. Irv applied just enough
pressure to turn him, then worked downstream and waded
out again into the water, where he netted a beautiful,
golden-bellied fish larger than anything I had in my creel.

The point is that Irv hadn't been fishing close enough
to the hides. Brown trout, especially those on heavily fished
streams, generally lie far under hides during sunny, daytime hours. They will not venture far from their protective
cover. Even a few inches make a vast difference.

But, back to terminal tackle. Here again, there has been
much experimenting, much discussion, some disagreement.
I lean to a three-hook worm gang similar to that used by
old Alec. Ivor and Dave Evans like a two-hook gang.
Ockie Swanson, another fine wormer, favors a single No. 8
hook buried in the nose of the small worms we use.

Regardless of the type of hook rig you use, there will
be little difference in the number of fish taken, provided
you have the right size of hook for the worm you are
using.

I remember a magnificent catch of browns Dave took
several years ago on worm gangs he tied with No. 20

hooks. He had very small pink worms, dug from clay. He took off alone early one morning around 3:00 A.M. Pictures of that catch appeared in several newspapers. Dave cautiously informed questioners that he had "been down on Mansfield Creek," a gin-clear problem stream with a reputation for big fish that couldn't be taken. The latter wasn't true. Our gang took many big fish on the Mansfield but Dave didn't take his whoppers there that day. He had been "down on" the Mansfield all right, but the mosquitoes were bad and Dave shifted operations quickly and made his big catch on Cattaraugus Creek, some miles away. He had three trout in the four to five-pound bracket— all on No. 20 hooks. He lost several more lunkers and released about a dozen fish of a size that would have made most any angler gleeful.

Sinkers probably cause more snagging problems than hooks. And proper sinkers are possibly the most vital link in the whole chain of your tackle. If you don't use sinkers properly, you may have mediocre results even though you equip yourself well and handle all your other equipment perfectly.

Old Alec used a dropper of silkworm gut, to which he pinched on BB shot. He could remove or add single shot easily when stream conditions suggested such a step and, for sure, Alec's technique was deadly. Our gang discovered that wrap-around lead sinkers in different thicknesses of metal and different lengths provide fewer snagging problems. The wrap-arounds are applied directly to the monofilament leader. It is extremely simple to remove the entire sinker or parts of it when stream conditions call for a change in weight.

chapter 3

Basic Technique

IN LEARNING WHY IT IS SO VITALLY NECESSARY TO USE sinkers properly, you will grasp one major reason why skillful worming is more difficult than any other type of trout angling. A worm fisherman must know far more about a stream than a fly man. He must understand and calculate not only top-water stream movements, but also varying currents as well as obstructions and snags at the bottom of the stream. In acquiring this detailed knowledge over a period of years, he can become a far more effective fly man.

The problems of the dry-fly man, for instance, probably are the simplest of all. After acquiring some stream knowledge and learning the mechanics of laying out a fly, his problems basically are confined to selection of the proper fly and preventing drag on that fly—on the surface, where he can easily watch it all the time.

The charm of watching all the action on the surface is great. I love a dry fly. I wouldn't consider anything else on Yellowstone-area streams or Montana's Big Hole or

Michigan's Au Sable or any other stream where insects
are the major summer food for trout. It would be unthinkable to use worms when you can have the pleasure
of watching a floating fly during the Au Sable's caddis-fly
hatch or during the Madison River's salmon-fly hatch.

The dry fly not only is more pleasurable to fish on such
waters, but you undoubtedly will have as much or more
action than you would have with a worm. On such streams,
where insects are plentiful, a skillful dry-fly man undoubtedly would outfish even a good wormer.

On the Missouri Flats of the Madison River one evening
last summer, I saw this fact demonstrated quite clearly.
There's a wooden bridge crossing the Madison on the Missouri Flats. At the bridge were the parked cars of at least
a half-dozen trout anglers. With field glasses, I watched
two better-than-average wormers working a white-water
stretch upstream. I learned later that they had been fishing all day. They were Salt Lake City men who had taken
many good fish with worms from the Madison before
flies started to appear.

But on that day and for several days previously, they
had taken only a few small trout while good dry-fly men
were returning with bulging creels. With the field glasses,
I admired the skill of two dry-fly men working through
the rushing water and boulders around a grassy island
several hundred yards downstream. These two were from
Chicago. One had the finest catch of brown trout I've
ever seen taken on a dry fly. Every one of his Loch Leven
(brown) trout weighed three pounds or more. One was
four and a half pounds.

They told me they had been taking fish like that on a
dry fly for the past week but that the salmon-fly hatch
now appeared to be over. Apparently it was. I tried a dry
fly the next day and took only one good fish, a twenty-
two incher, but wormers didn't do as well.

If all this seems besides the point, it isn't. Some streams clearly are fly streams. These, generally, are streams not subject to spring freshets so violent that they destroy most of the insect life. Most fly streams are in heavily wooded sections where trees and plant life prevent a rapid runoff of snow or rain.

In streams subject to rapid runoffs, particularly streams in the more populated sections of the East, trout depend less on stream insects for food and more on minnows, crayfish, worms, grasshoppers, and the like.

It is on streams like this that the skillful wormer becomes king. He also has much more action and more pleasure without necessarily killing any more fish. While worming—and this is the point of the discussion on dryflies—he'll learn more about water currents and trout hides in a few years than he could in a lifetime of fly angling.

A consistently successful wormer must know the water he is fishing from surface to bottom. He must judge the speed of the current at all levels with great precision. From telltale boils and eddies that show on the surface, he learns to judge accurately the position and general nature of boulders and logs on the bottom. He learns to judge depth of the water.

All these things he must learn, in addition to general stream knowledge, to become a good wormer. Those underwater factors are of far less importance to the fly man. Even the wet-fly man's lure generally is only a few inches under the surface. Only the good nymph man has problems similar to the wormer, and top-notch nymph men are as rare as top-notch wormers.

The highly important sinker is the tool with which you solve the problems of depth and speed of water.

In approaching any trout hide with a short line and a worm, the likely position of a hiding trout must be considered with great care, especially if your worm must

negotiate snag-ridden water. Even fly men must try to determine where trout are lying in order to do an effective
job. That's part of general stream lore. Unlike fly presenta-
tion, however, the worm should first be seen by the trout
as it wiggles along the bottom. A second cast, after poor
initial placing of the worm, is far less effective. Make a
cast that causes stream-wise trout to suspect there's something fishy in Denmark and your chance of taking that fish
is small. You must do it right the first time for each drift.

To place that worm properly in relation to the trout's
suspected hiding place takes a little study. Even longtime
wormers will study stream speed, depth, and the telltale
boils of underwater obstructions before making a cast. The
all-important objective is to have the worm sink to the
bottom several feet upstream from the hide and then
dribble within darting range of the trout. That is simpler
said than done.

If your worm sinks to the bottom too far upstream
from the trout's lair, the chances are good that your sinker
or worm will lodge under a rock or sunken twig before
the worm drifts into the trout's range. If your worm is
placed so closely to the trout's hide that it is first seen as
something plunging rapidly and unnaturally from the surface to the bottom, you can depend on it that the red-
warning flashers will start blinking in the trout's super-
sensitive nervous system.

A fish so skilled that it can dart out unerringly into
twisting currents and invariably intercept tiny insects
would know without doubt that a rapidly sinking worm
was a phony. Only a small and foolish trout would take
a worm presented in such a way.

So, the problem is to place the worm upstream at such
a point that it will sink to the bottom just upstream from
the fish and still be able to move naturally downstream.

That means a nice combination of accurate placing of the worm in relation to the speed of the current and depth of the water, and good judgment in the weight of the sinker to do the job.

If the current is swift and the sinker light, obviously you would have to drop your worm much farther upstream in order to permit it to reach the bottom before the worm reached the fish. If the current is swift and you use a sinker that is too heavy, the worm will move too slowly along the bottom. The chances are that it will stop completely. Such a stoppage also would be unnatural, unless it is only momentary.

Each hide presents a different problem for the wormer who properly considers whether the sinker on his line is of the right weight. If he deems the sinker too light, he'll wrap another section of lead around his leader. If he believes the sinker too heavy, he'll tear off part of the lead strip. Sinker changes are made frequently. There's plenty of time for that because there should be a waiting period after the approach to a hide.

Learning how to approach wary trout closely is an art in itself, something that few fly men every try to learn. Most fly men rely on casting long lines to solve that problem. They lose a great deal by so doing. A short line usually will do a better job for a dry-fly man if his approach is good. The shorter the line, the fewer problems of fly drag. We'll discuss the approach at more length later.

There is no doubt that there are stream situations that call for a long line. Sometimes a long line will pay off handsomely with a worm, just as it will sometimes with a dry fly. Using either a regular fly line or monofilament, several of our gang can roll cast or shoot worms as far as seventy feet upstream. The use of such a long line usually is confined to large pools that couldn't be fished out properly with a short line, or glassy pools that prevent a close approach—without being seen by the fish—no matter what kind of approach you can make.

The occasional need for a long line is one reason why I like the closed fly-rod type of spinning reel. I like the side opening on the left side and the handle on the right so I can use the reel effectively with a short line. I find that the line catches frequently on a left-handed reel. This not only is annoying: it can be downright embarrassing if a trout should happen to strike at that moment.

The closed fly-rod type of spinning reel also permits the effective use of "hardware," which, under certain conditions, will outfish even a worm. With this reel, you don't have to go back to your tackle box in the car to get another reel if you want to switch from worming to spinning.

Nowhere, so far, have I described our worming methods for upstream worming. Actually, the method requires upstream wading but, considering the short line normally used, the cast usually is cross-stream or up and across at an angle, always with the rod tip as directly downstream from the worm as possible. It is difficult to use a short line and fish directly upstream without frightening trout at many points in your upstream progress. In cross-stream angling, the worm is lifted slowly and gently from the water as soon as it reaches a downstream position in which it drags or lifts from the bottom.

You can cast directly or quartering upstream only with a longer line, but the longer line usually requires a lighter sinker or the rig will tend to catch unnaturally on the bottom. When a long line seems desirable and your cast is quartering upstream, hold the rod as far out into the stream as possible to place the tip directly below the worm. At the same time, strip in enough line to prevent excessive slack.

While it might seem, at first glance, that it would be difficult to avoid drag when fishing cross-stream, it is simple with a short line. Let's say your rod is ten feet long and your line ten feet. The length of your extended arm will add another two feet or more.

You approach a hide, regardless of width of stream—assuming that depth of water is not prohibitive—and cast upstream to a point that will bring your worm in very close to where you figure a trout may be hiding. Then, holding your arm extended so that you get the maximum advantage from your long rod, you follow the line downstream with your tip, always holding the tip a few inches downstream from the point where your line enters the water. If you don't keep the tip downstream from the line, you will get a drag that will cause the worm to lift from the bottom or move more slowly than it would if unhampered.

If your line is slanting away from your rod tip toward the opposite bank or a hide, you will have an unnatural across-the-current drag of the worm, unless you are able to throw slack line and the current speed is approximately the same both at the point where your worm is drifting and where your line is slanting through the water.

Try to avoid a slanting line. Sometimes, particularly on big water, it is unavoidable. When you do have a slanting line, throw as much slack as possible to minimize drag. Some slack line usually can be thrown by quickly lowering the rod tip toward the water.

Strange as it may seem, certain hides are fished more effectively downstream. Take a hide in which a large tree has fallen into a stream and is held there by large rocks or its own weight. The branches will project far upstream from the spot you figure a trout is most likely to hide—under the trunk of the tree near the far bank, we'll assume.

It would be unthinkable to fish that hide from the far bank, unless you want to do as the worm-dunkers do. You just couldn't get a natural float. Furthermore, by fishing from a standing position over the fish, you'd make yourself clearly visible. So you position yourself upstream from the tree branches and fish downstream.

It is possible, and not at all difficult, to make the worm float naturally in such a situation, provided you properly select the point at which to drop your worm and the amount of slack line to throw. If you can get by with a short line and still reach to and slightly below the hide before drag will appear, you can make your cast with the rod held high; then lower your rod smoothly at such a speed that it permits a slight downstream belly in the line at a point just downstream from the position of the worm. The worm always will move a little slower than the line because it will be catching on the bottom. With this type of cast, your selection of sinker weight must be well considered. Unless the water is rushing, you'll tend to use too heavy a sinker and it will catch on the bottom and spoil a natural float. That often will end your chances in that pool for the time being.

As always, there are exceptions but, generally, two good casts to a hide are all you should make. If a fish doesn't take in two good casts, the chances are he'll not take in a dozen or more. In fact, I've had the theory that, after two good casts, further casting will make that trout more difficult to raise if you want to try for him later in the day. In any event, nagging the fish with a worm doesn't seem to help. It isn't like creating a "hatch" with a dry fly. Cast twice, maybe three times, then spend your time more productively on another fish. Move along, if only a few feet. Don't waste your time on a fish that needs to be nagged—unless you know the fish is a big one.

Exceptions to that rule include hides so large and varied that you cannot cover the entire hide with a few drifts, and days during which rain has discolored the water. When water is discolored or when a stream has been lightly fished for a long period, trout are much more inclined to come out of their hides and feed in open riffles and shallows quite some distance from their usual lurking places.

Ivor Evans convinced me one warm, rainy day years ago, that fishing close in to hides during periods of discolored water often is inadvisable. I had been doing just that. Because I could not see the underwater snags, I had been losing much fishing time replacing lost rigs. When I met Ivor for lunch at the car that day, he had more and better fish than I. There was a reason. Ivor hadn't been one-tracked as I had been. His method was to cast upstream so that the worm would float down in unobstructed water as far as twenty feet from the hide. The next cast would bring the worm down about eighteen feet from the hide. The casts would come closer and closer until he'd get a strike.

After some experimentation in colored water, Ivor came to the conclusion—and I've since found it to be true—that if you find several trout at a distance of, say, five feet from the usual hangouts, you'll probably find the majority of fish on that stream at that time at about the same distance from their hides. It is amazing how closely all trout on a stream tend to follow the same pattern of location and feeding preferences at any given time.

Fishing in this way, Ivor lost far less tackle, had more fishing time, and took more fish. But note well that this away-from-the-hide fishing applies primarily to discolored water. When fishing clear water, Polaroid glasses help greatly to spot the densest thickets of snags.

chapter 4

Taking Trout
on Crowded Streams

THE SUN WAS GLARING ONE HOT JULY DAY SEVERAL YEARS ago. Dozens of trout anglers had pounded every likely pool on Western New York's Wiscoy throughout the morning, using wet, dry, and streamer flies as well as worms, minnows, and grasshoppers. A few nice fish had been taken early in the morning but, as the temperature rose into the eighties, action virtually ceased. By noon, most of the anglers had quit or gone back to their cars.

There'd been a social gathering with cocktails the night before and we hadn't arrived at the stream until late in the morning. The lateness didn't concern me. Taking a limit catch of nice fish after other anglers had thrashed through all the good water is common practice for our gang. I was a little worried, however, by the heat and more so by the lack of breeze. Without a breeze to create ripples and partly conceal our movements from the fish, the problem of approaching a glassy pool becomes increasingly difficult.

As we pulled into the shade at the top of a high bank a few miles below the village of Pike, several groups of anglers lolled about on the ground. Several of them gazed fondly at cans of beer. A few unseen warblers sang from the tops of overhanging trees but their calls seemed a little dispirited. The heat apparently was getting them, too.

Harry Coxon, a wonderful companion who died just before publication of this book, was with me.

There was no friend to whom I tried harder to teach the fine points of worm angling than Harry Coxon. He knew every point. He knew how to apply everything told him. Yet, he and many other friends I'd tried to teach seemed incapable of retaining all the necessary requirements to successful worming at all times. If you reminded him of one thing he was doing improperly, he'd correct that and forget another. I suspect Harry didn't care too much whether he caught many fish or not. He loved to be afield, to commune with nature and he'd rely on me to satisfy his fondness for a mess of trout.

Our car had hardly stopped when Harry eased himself out of the front seat and sidled smilingly over to one of the sitting groups. Within a minute, he was doing all the talking. Furthermore, the group was enjoying Harry, as I did. They gave each of us a can of beer. We drank the liquid slowly. In that heat, we felt no hurry. Far down the bank through the trees I could see the sun's glare on the water.

It must have been nearly an hour before we trudged down the trail to the bank of the Wiscoy. I sat on a log, lit a cigarette and suggested to Harry that he start upstream. After a little interval, I would follow.

My perspiring feet and legs felt almost wet as the sun toasted my boots. I waded into the stream, sat on a dry boulder and let my feet dangle in the water.

I knew there would be no point in fishing obvious or easy-to-reach places. Every one of these had been pounded throughout the morning. All the fish that had been lying in these places either had been taken, or, more likely, frightened back deep under the hides from which they had come. At this time of day, also, every hungry trout would probably be in the shade, even though that shade might be only an overhanging rock.

Early in the mornings and on dark days, it is quite common to hook good trout in open water, particularly where riffles break into pools. But when the sun is shining brightly and a stream has been fished heavily before you have reached it, it is an almost invariable rule, virtually inflexible on smaller streams, that brown trout will be lying under something.

This might be anything from an overhanging bank or a rock to a clump of bushes or a log. The trout must feel safe from its many enemies, most of which attack from above. Usually, it will lie in relatively quiet water only a few inches from its bread basket—the current sweeping by with assorted food.

Give a trout an overhead cover and it will be quite content in only a few inches of water. It's important to be aware of this when you fish heavily pounded streams. The amateur is the one who looks only for deep pools. The expert frequently takes many of his fish, often large fish, from water so shallow that it would be passed up completely by all but stream-wise anglers.

When I started upstream after Harry, it was the shallow water I studied, particularly along the high banks on the far side of the stream. Hundreds of anglers had walked out a wide path along the low banks and virtually all the angling was done from that side. Occasionally the low banks would shift from one side of the stream to the other.

Then the anglers' path would cross a shallow riffle. Only a few rank tyros ever try to fish from the top of the high banks, where every movement they make is seen by trout below.

On a pounded stream of this type, most anglers follow approximately the same pattern. They'll see a nice-looking stretch from the bank, wade a little way into the stream and fish out the stretch. Then they'll wade back to the bank and walk along it until they come to another good-looking stretch where this procedure will be repeated.

So, unless you know you are the first man fishing a stream that day, concentrate on stretches of water that you're pretty sure have been passed up by the other fellow. That was one of Alec Henderson's tricks.

I hadn't moved upstream along the bank more than a few hundred feet from the boulder on which I had been sitting, when I spotted a little curl of current near the opposite bank, where the tip of an overhanging bush was waving gently in the water. A small clump of dead grass was clinging to the tip of the bush. The water was no more than three or four inches deep. I had to wade some forty feet over slippery stones to reach the spot.

The water movement was slow and I removed most of my sinker. I waited a few minutes to let the water quiet down. I had seen small wakes of water, caused by my wading, sweep into the hide. This, obviously, was a warning signal to any stream-wise trout. The fish should have a little time to forget about it. Meanwhile, I studied the stream currents just upstream from the hide.

I made sure that the small worm only dimpled the surface of the water as I eased it in gently about four feet directly up-current from the hide. I made two casts. There was no response but I wasn't disappointed. You don't find hungry trout in every hide. Nevertheless, this was exactly the kind of pocket I was looking for. I'd find many more like it and I was pretty sure I'd take fish from some of them.

I came to a lovely pool. Back in WPA days, the CCC had built a log wall on this bend of the Wiscoy to prevent erosion. The roots of a fallen tree had caught in the wall and the tree trunk and branches hung downstream, paralleling the CCC wall.

The edge of the tree trunk was roughly a foot from the wall and some vagrant twigs projecting from the tree trunk cut off the channel. A worm could be drifted only a few feet.

I knew that everyone on the stream that day probably had fished the pool which the log had created.

The center of the pool and the portion of it near the log were a cinch to fish with any type of lure. I didn't even bother to make a cast there. I walked downstream to a point where the water was shallow, permitting me to reach a bar in the center of the stream. Then I worked upstream again, around the tree branches lying in the water and took up a position from which I could cast a short line into the channel between the CCC wall and the tree trunk. The water was fairly deep, the current quite swift. I added a half-coil of sinker. The cast had to be right on the button.

I felt the light catching of the sinker along the bottom, then a thrilling, pulsating throb. I struck, then realized that this was a fish I probably never would land. In effect, my line was in a barrel and the fish was too heavy to haul over the top of the log. But that's something you don't worry about. Attain the satisfaction of making hard-to-catch trout strike, then worry about landing them after you've hooked them.

It was a good fish, possibly a pound, and I lost it and

my terminal tackle. I replaced the tackle. The lost fish convinced me that the heat hadn't caused the trout to go into a sulk and my confidence rose.

Just upstream from the riffle running into the CCC wall was a large clump of alders. Interlaced branches hung over and into the water for a distance of about ten feet from the far bank. The current past the tips of these branches was swift and I knew no trout normally would lie in such a current. The fast water was evident under the branches almost to the far bank. I could see the stream had cut under the alder roots. There was no way to make a cast through the branches. Here was a situation that would be impossible without light monofilament line. I was using four-pound test line that day, with a six-foot tip of two-pound test.

The memory of how I lost the last fish tormented me a bit, so I jockeyed around until I found a channel in the underwater branches through which I could lead a fish in case I hooked one. There still wasn't any possibility of a cast. I worked up near the downstream tips of the alder clump, lightened my sinker, and shortened the leader from the tip of my rod to about twelve inches. I coiled about ten feet of line in my left hand and pushed the tip of the rod carefully through the branches. When the tip of the rod was several feet upstream from the pocket in which I figured a trout might lie, I released the coil of monofilament in my hand. The combined weight of sinker and worm pulled the line out smoothly through the guides. The worm slid into the water and a trout snapped it up almost instantly. I struck as hard as I dared, at the same time backing away from the alders. Then I succeeded in leading the trout through the brushy tangle into open water.

I've found that even large trout may be drawn out from

such difficult spots without too much trouble if you do it decisively and powerfully as soon as you strike. In fact, the strike and drawing motion are made at the same time. You get the fish coming before it has a chance to know what is happening.

This particular fish came out of the tangle without too much trouble but it was a powerful fish and determined to get back to its lair. I tried to keep it upstream from me in the fast water sweeping past the tips of the bushes, but quickly realized that if I stayed in my present position, almost directly downstream, I couldn't keep the fish from moving sideways into the tangle. I splashed over to the gravel bar across from the alders so I could apply more direct strain against the tangle-bound boring of the fish. I stepped into a hole and felt pleasingly-cool water trickle down the inside of my hot boots.

Then the fish swung abruptly downstream toward the riffle leading to the CCC wall and the log. The monofilament line raced out of my reel. I ran along the bank. The fish swung again and headed back toward its lair. It leaped and I saw it clearly for the first time. In my mind, I can still see the deeply-etched black spots, the deep gold of its belly. The trout rolled again, then started to drift downstream to my waiting net.

It was a nice fish, around seventeen inches, and its weight felt good in my creel as I started upstream again. I came to a shallow stretch with fairly high banks on both sides of the stream. I slid into the water. A high bank is no place for a trout fisherman unless he plans to use a long line. I saw a pocket under an overhanging maple on the opposite side of the stream, where a few dead twigs had lodged in the bottom. Between me and that pocket was a glassy stretch of water only a few inches deep.

As I approached the pocket, quartering upstream, I

crouched low. Then I got to my knees and inched along, using one hand on the stream bottom to help my progress. I looked down and saw the shallow water curling danger-ously near the top of my boots. My sinker seemed about right. I waited a few minutes to let the water quiet down.

Upstream a little ways, a kingfisher chattered, then plunged into a quiet pool and came up with a little chub. I could feel the sun burning the side of my face and wondered whether my sensitive skin would peel again.

I cast. The cast was a bad one. It was about a foot too far upstream and the line stopped several feet short of the pocket. I raised my rod tip gently and knew I was snagged on something. I pointed the rod tip at the snagged hook and broke the line free. I stuck the rod butt in a pocket of my fishing vest and, still on my knees, tied on another tippet, sinker and three-hook gang. This time I used more care in my cast and the worm floated nicely into the pocket. The line throbbed. Somehow I always get a thrill from that throb, a thrill almost as great as I get from the rise of a trout to a dry fly. Maybe it's the momentary mystery of what may be on the end of your line. This time it was a small trout, just about minimum legal size, maybe a little smaller. The trout had taken the hooks deeply, although it had not swallowed them, and I snipped off the leader where it entered the trout's mouth and released the fish.

Then, still on my knees, I saw another tiny pocket near the base of the overhanging tree. It didn't look too good but it was a possible hide. I tied on another hook, slipping the sinker up on the cut-off leader to my favored position, about six to eight inches from the hook. I cast again.

In the shallow water, I clearly saw a nice trout race out from the pocket to meet the worm and dash back into the hide, the worm in its mouth. The fish thrashed wildly but didn't leap. Except for its own pocket and the little pile of brush, it had no traps about which I had to worry. I let the fish tire itself and slid a twelve incher into the net. I knew Harry wanted fish for expected guests and kept it.

Interesting opportunities to fish places that most anglers skip, presented themselves at close intervals all along the stream. I met five die-hard anglers who had kept fishing in spite of the tough fishing conditions and the heat. Only two of these had fish, several small ones each.

I came to a setup that is always interesting under hot-weather conditions. A cold brook ran into the stream. There was no pool below the brook, however, and I guessed that most anglers had passed up this spot. About twenty-five feet downstream from the brook was a log. Most of it was imbedded in mud, but under the end jut-ting out into the stream was an opening through which water was moving. The water depth at this point probably wasn't over three inches. Yet, from under that log, I lured a fish of about a pound.

I made no other casts at the hides where I had caught fish. Only rarely will you catch a second trout after the water has been disturbed by the frantic efforts of one trout to escape. Better to move on and find new pockets.

When I caught up with Harry, I had seven trout in creel, none under ten inches. I had released three or four more around ten inches, plus several more around seven inches. On a tough day like that, I felt thoroughly satisfied.

Harry's face was red and perspiring. There were dark patches of perspiration on his shirt around his armpits. He had four fish over our own minimum size of ten inches.

"Had a lot of damn sinker strikes," Harry complained.

I knew what he meant. I had several such strikes myself. You can determine whether you've had a sinker strike easily. You get the decisive throb on your line and you strike, but you usually feel the fish for only a moment. Then, when you inspect your worm, you'll find it untouched. The reason is obvious. The coil sinkers appear to the fish like the segments of nymph larvae. A good nymph fisherman would have taken these fish.

We had enough fish and decided to experiment. We wrapped a coil of lead on a small, long-shanked hook and dropped down to a long, uninteresting-looking run about six inches deep, where Harry said he had had several sinker strikes. We cast our lead sinkers, fishing them exactly as we would a worm and, giggling like kids, succeeded in taking and releasing several small trout each. If nothing else, it indicates to me that the presence of a coil sinker on a leader certainly does not harm your chances. Since I've realized that, I've tended, more and more, to lower the sinker closer to the hook. I'm now convinced that the sinker is more of an attraction than a necessary weighting device.

The foregoing account of an actual day on a crowded stream in hot weather, describes only a few of the many types of hides for which you should look and the ways in which you should fish them. Each stream, each day, has special problems. To fish successfully, you can do nothing by mere rote. You, and you alone, must solve the interesting problems as they arise.

chapter 5

Small Worms vs. Nightcrawlers

THE DIRECTOR OF ONE OF THE LARGEST ART MUSEUMS IN the country, in keeping with his position, is a very correct man when he is among patrons of the arts or among strangers. In fact, he may give you the impression of being downright stuffy. But he loves trout fishing and, until he learned a better way of doing it, he felt quite strongly that there was no other way to fish a worm than dunking a nightcrawler in a deep hole and holding it there with a heavy sinker. In some ways, his attitude was typical of that of the average worm dunker, who tries hard, usually takes few trout.

"Why, Mr. Wood, it only makes good sense to assume that a trout would prefer a large morsel of food and wouldn't relish pursuing it," he expounded with precise enunciation, as he, Pem Shober, and I drove out to Clear Creek in Wyoming County on a warm, showery morning late one May. His comment was made after I had sug-

44

gested he might like to try to learn floating a small worm.

We'll call him Mr. A. When Pem introduced us that morning, I guessed pretty quickly that Mr. A. was much too gifted and literate a person for me. I felt sure I couldn't come anywhere near his high standards.

All the way out to the stream, except for the few minutes of dissertation on the merits of nightcrawlers, Mr. A. discussed art, poetry, sculpture. He insisted on addressing me as "Mr. Wood," instead of the "Jerry" I requested. Even while carrying on a dissertation on worm-dunking, his speech was meticulous. He never cussed, not even mildly. I never heard a slang word. He was attired in perfectly pressed trousers, a white shirt and bow tie, a neat tan jacket. His rimless eyeglasses sparkled under a gray dress hat. I became a little uneasy. I just couldn't stay on a high plane with this fellow for a whole day and get much fun out of it.

Mr. A. was very polite and gentlemanly in urging Pem and me to use nightcrawlers. He and Pem had been friends for years but this was the first time they had been fishing together. So, Mr. A., much more concerned with his art gallery, wasn't aware of the newer methods our gang was developing. Pem wasn't an early member of the gang but he was working hard learning.

Anyway, I figured out a way to get away from culture for a few hours at least. I asked them to put me off at a bridge in the village of Arcade and suggested they go upstream a mile or so to the next bridge. I'd meet them there around noon.

Actually, the water they had to fish was much better. Stream conditions were ideal for dunking. A warm rain during the night had colored Clear Creek, normally one of the most translucent streams I've ever encountered. It is a stream well known throughout Western New York as a real problem stream, but the home of many lunkers. A pond that is its source has yielded several national prize-winning browns.

As I worked through the village, then out into an open flat containing only a few, isolated willows and sycamores, I realized that this was going to be a good day. I enjoyed the patter of the warm rain on my raincoat and I began to relax from the strain of trying to be literate and gentle-manly. Trout came fast and easy. I released at least a dozen good fish. I kept several fish of about two pounds each, one of three and a half pounds and several more that weighed well over a pound.

I wondered how Mr. A. was doing with his dunking and figured that, if there ever was a day in which dunk-ing would be successful, this was it. I confess to a sneaky hope that he wouldn't be able to prove his point. The rain stopped and a weak sun shone through the clouds. I re-moved my raincoat and continued upstream. Then I came upon Mr. A.

"Well, Mr. Wood, I trust you have been successful," Mr. A. called out cheerily. How do you like that for a greeting to a trout fisherman, especially when it was de-livered in his best pontifical manner. I squirmed and mut-tered something about catching a few.

"How you doin'," I asked. To me, his smile indicated he was pleased with himself. I wondered if the discolored waters had given him a chance to lecture further on the merits of nightcrawlers. Then I became a little sorry when he told me he had taken two trout of about nine inches each. He was restrained in his pride but obviously quite pleased with himself.

He asked nothing further about my catch as we worked up to the car. Pem had been fishing upstream and he was walking toward us when we arrived. I threw my creel, net and fishing vest into the trunk of the car. Pem couldn't wait until he got to us before he reached in his creel and, with a little boy's enthusiasm, displayed a gorgeous, hook-nosed brown which we later weighed in at four pounds, two ounces. It was the only fish Pem caught, but that one fish was more than enough.

Pem, his hands still shaking, dragged out a quart-size thermos bottle of martinis. We celebrated and heard all the details of Pem's catch. He had hooked it in a riffle just above a deep pool and must have had a devil of a time keeping it out of the snags in the pool. At one time, the fish did hook up in the snags but Pem got the fish started again by rapping sharply on the rod butt while he held a taut line.

The martinis started to take effect. Pem was buoyant. He started to sing a racy Scottish song in dialect. No one can surpass Pem in his loose imitations of the speech of Europeans. Then we sat in the car, the doors open, and started to eat our lunches. The martinis not withstanding, Mr. A. still was meticulously polite. His sole concession to the martinis was a humorous poem that bordered on the risque. Then he almost bolted upright as a thought struck him.

"Why, Mr. Wood, we haven't even seen your trout," he exclaimed. "They're back in the trunk," I replied, as casually as I could. "I would say we have been very impolite," Mr. A. regretted, turning to Pem as a partner in crime. "Let us see them immediately."

He and Pem got out and walked to the rear of the car. I followed, munching on a sandwich. Mr. A. lifted the lid of the creel, without moving it from the floor of the trunk. One of my smaller fish was partly buried in grass at the top.

"Why, Mr. Wood, this fish is simply grand," Mr. A.

beamed. "Oh my, here's another magnificent specimen. See here, Pemberton, look at this one. My, oh my!"

Then, as he started to reach the larger fish, his face reddened. He groaned, looked at Pem with an almost-hurt expression, then at me and shouted loudly:

"You two dirty, rotten stinkers."

From then on, Mr. A. was a regular guy. In fact, he was a peach. I was surprised to learn that he could cuss easily when the occasion called for it and his store of knowledge went far beyond art. He dropped his excessive politeness, his precise enunciation. At heart, he was a swell joe, with most of his fine down-to-earth qualities bottled up in a job-created shell.

For the rest of the day, his sole interest was in learning the techniques Pem and I had used. He was so eager, so excited that I decided to take him in tow. I hadn't planned to fish any more that day, anyway. I already had far more fish than I usually keep.

We moved to a bridge about two miles upstream. I handed Mr. A. my rod and started off with him. He was an enthusiastic pupil but he just couldn't seem to place the worm accurately in pockets that I suggested. He had difficulty avoiding line drag. But after a while he did succeed in snagging into a fat fourteen-incher. That made him a happy man. To my knowledge, he's never dunked a nightcrawler for trout since.

This is not to say that a nightcrawler does not have its place. Our gang refuses to use them, but there are a very few times when a dunked nightcrawler will do a better job than a floated worm that has been dug from loam or clay or, in a pinch, taken from leaf piles.

I recall a day late in April some years ago when I fished Ischua Creek with Art Itzenplitz and his son, Chuck. Both were confirmed lake fishermen but Art had seen some of our gang's catches of trout in previous years. They had a can of nightcrawlers. Lake Erie still was too cold for fishing and they had that same urge that hits most of us as soon as the ice and snow start to disappear in spring. You just have to bust out of your stuffy winter cocoon, to celebrate the coming of spring by getting some fresh air in your nostrils.

I made a few suggestions to Art and Chuck as we drove to the Ischua but advised them that the floating of a worm in the cold waters of early spring is uncertain at best. In cold water, brown trout remain semi-dormant. They will not move more than a few inches for a worm. When they do move, they do it slowly, deliberately. They tend to avoid fast water.

They are more likely to lie in quiet pools or in sluggish eddies at the edge of fast water. The water often is slightly discolored and the browns are less insistent on overhead cover. I've just about quit brown trout fishing in spring until the waters warm up, until all traces of snow have disappeared, until most of the spring eager-beavers have disappeared from the streams and hied themselves to some lake or pond where panfish are plentiful.

It was some years ago that I spent the day with Art and Chuck Itzenplitz. I stayed with them a little while to give them some idea of how to float a worm and then started up the creek. When I returned several hours later, both of them were sitting on the bank of the pool. I had taken only two small trout. They grinned at me and I asked them if they had had any luck.

Without a word, Art reached into a cloth bag beside him and pulled out four good-sized trout. Chuck, on the other side of the pool, had taken six. All the fish had been taken by dunking their nightcrawlers. They hadn't had a strike while floating a worm.

Some wormers assume that their type of angling comes
to an end when waters become clear and low. As soon as
mosquitoes start to bite, as soon as an alder leaf becomes
as large as a mouse's ear, these wormers figure they've had
it for the season. Usually, these wormers are dunkers. Actually, the finest worm angling of all is enjoyed in the
hot summer months.

There usually is a short period in June, during the first
hot days, when a drifted worm will produce only fair
results. There often is another such period after the first
cool spell late in August. During those short periods, I
suspect the trout are concentrating on minnows or the
few insects or larvae in the streams. Of course we are
talking about the freshet type of streams that predominate
in the East.

In those first hot June days, you will notice more minnows in the quiet eddies of many eastern streams than at
any other time of the summer.

This is their time for a spring coming-out party. The
trout take advantage of it. For about a week, the minnow
fisherman will have a heyday. After that, the good wormer
will come back into his own and, throughout the summer,
almost invariably outfish anglers using any other type of
lure or bait. On most streams, he'll even outfish a grasshopper man in grasshopper time.

In those June and late-August periods, there is no sense
in trying to cram worms down the throats of balky trout
when other pleasurable methods of taking them are at
hand.

In the June period, I do one of two things. I switch
either to a dry fly or a spinning rod. There is no type of
trout fishing I enjoy more than a dry fly and, after all,
I need an opportunity to toughen up my casting wrist
for vacation fishing on far-away fly waters. Somehow,

although I believe the trout concentrate on minnows in that June period, the small ones will take a dry fly readily and I enjoy this fishing immensely. Most of the fish taken on the dry fly, however, are not worth keeping. I release virtually all of them. I balk at wet flies for trout. They are far less productive than worms, less fun to fish.

If I want some trout to eat, I'll hook up a spinning rod, but there'll be more on that later. I use nothing but a spinning rod on eastern streams late in the summer. At this time, as the big trout start to fatten up for their semi-hibernation in winter, you will take more big trout with a properly fished spinning lure than in any other way.

Even far-away streams that normally are most enjoyable when fished with a fly, often become moody. There will be days in a row in which fly fishermen do little or nothing. These include such streams as New York State's Ausable, Beaverkill and Esopus. When I get skunked or nearly skunked with a fly for several days in a row on such streams, I bow to better judgment and dig out my worming gear. It seldom fails me.

There is a certain stretch on the Ausable, downstream from Wilmington, that has been kinder to me than any other stretch of water in the East. It is a rare day on that stretch when I can't catch a limit of fair fish on a dry fly. At one point a cold brook flows into the main stream. On the hottest of days, I almost invariably can take trout just downstream from the point where that brook enters. On such days, in fact, the trout concentrate there.

I introduced Frank Avery and Joe Rigler to that stretch a few years ago. It is in an isolated section, a good distance from the road and you seldom see another angler there. The day before the three of us had dry-flied to death a picturesque, white-water stretch upstream from the Wilmington Notch campsite. Since we didn't catch enough

trout together to feed one of our families, I took them to
my ace-in-the-hole stretch.

There wasn't room on the section for three of us so I
told them to fish it while I drove on a few miles further
to a brook where I had taken several nice trout the year
before. I agreed to return with the car around 2:00 P.M.
The temperature was in the eighties.

Frank and I used dry flies that day but Joe switched to
a worm. Joe is a busy plant foreman and he doesn't have
too much time for trout except during vacations. Conse-
quently, he has much to learn about worming. Anyway,
when I returned with the car, Frank and Joe were sitting
at the side of the road, poking grass stems into their teeth.

"This is a helluva hot spot," Joe griped. "Cripes, from
the way you talked, I thought the stretch would be loaded
with trout. There isn't a damned trout in the whole stretch.
Come on, break down and take us where you take your
friends."

I was on the spot. Between them, Joe and Frank had
taken only three small trout. I also had three but my fish
were larger.

"Hell, you dump us off on a lousy stretch so you can
fish the good places yourself," Frank growled.

The ribbing continued the rest of that day. Even our
wives had to hear the details around the campfire that
night. I was on the defensive and I had to do something.
So I proposed my usual maximum bet of a nickel with both
Joe and Frank that I could take a limit of trout, ten inches
or better, from the much-maligned stretch on the following day. That gave them more ammunition. They tried
to get me to raise the bet. I had a hard time that evening.

Next morning I succeeded in buying one hundred
worms of the type I like the best from a farm boy on a

side road near Wilmington. Frank and Joe fished the brook I had fished the day before.

I had to release about a dozen fish under ten inches before I won my 10 cents that day. I had my limit of fish ranging to eighteen inches shortly after noon, virtually all of them taken from under snag-ridden boulders near the center of the stream. I lost many tackles.

There was a similar experience with worms on the Beaverkill only last year. My wife and I were returning from a business trip to New York City late in June and decided to stop off at Roscoe for a few days.

Dry flies produced few fish for me on the Beaverkill the first day. Other anglers, fishing both dry and wet flies, did little better. The next morning, I tried dry flies again. I caught only a few chubs.

After lunch, I drove to a stretch several miles upstream from Roscoe. Three carloads of anglers were standing around talking. There were only a few trout among them. Most of them were planning to wait for the evening hatch before expending any more energy.

We were leaving the next morning and I wanted to take home a few fish so—you guessed it. I acquired some worms and went to work. I returned to that bridge before 4:00 P.M. with the limit. Some of the men with whom I talked at noon still were there, lolling on grass along the road. They inquired about my luck, then asked to see the fish.

In the group was one professorial dry-fly purist who lost interest completely when I informed the group the trout had been taken on worms. The others pressed for details about equipment and methods. One carload of anglers was off to get some worms within five minutes after I returned.

chapter 6

Reels, Lines, and Leaders

For worm fishing only, there is nothing better than a simple, single-action reel. For most trout fishing, any reel is simply a line holder. A whopper fish might burn out a cheap reel with long runs, but for most waters inexpensive single-action reels will do a perfectly satisfactory job. Short-line casting usually gives the reel very little to do. My primary requirement in a worming reel is a minimum of doo-dads on which a line can catch when you are shooting it or throwing slack.

A catching line is a particular problem when fishing in a strong wind. You will always hold your line in the left hand (assuming that you are right-handed) and pay out and withdraw line with this hand as conditions warrant. A cross wind throwing a loop of line over a reel projection, particularly a left-handed handle, can ruin many good casts or drifts. For worming, the protruding left-handed handle on most spinning reels is an abomination.

I mentioned earlier a type of reel which does a good, if not perfect, job on both worming and spinning. This is the fly-rod type of closed spinning reel, with opening on the left side and handle on the right. In addition to spinning, this type of reel sometimes is handy for long, underhand casts with a worm. With this type of reel, there sometimes are mechanical annoyances or line tangles inside the reel if you don't make a point of keeping a reasonably taut line while worming. When you become familiar with such a reel's weaknesses, however, it is an excellent compromise. For worming only, use a single-action reel. For spinning only, you can't beat a top-grade, open-spool reel with a fast rate of retrieve. We'll explain the desirability of a rapid retrieve in a spinning reel later.

Our gang has experimented with lines and leaders through the entire range of types and diameters. Make no mistake about it; in clear water, the finer the leader and line, the more trout. This fact applies almost as surely to worming as it does to fly fishing, although an extremely light leader in worming is less important on most waters.

In worming, you have one big factor that inclines you toward a leader heavier than you would like to use. It is a factor with which fly fishermen do not have to reckon. In dribbling your worm along in the snag-ridden places in which most brown trout live, you will hook up many times each day on rocks, roots, sunken twigs, and the like.

If you are using a 4X tippet, such a leader will give you little strength with which to pull the hook or sinker free from snags. The tippet will even snap in bringing a sinker out from under a small rock. You find yourself losing many more tackles. The latter may be and should be thoroughly unimportant, but the time you lose fishing out new rigs and tying them on is very important. So all of our gang has sought a happy compromise. We still use 4X tips, even 5X, on some waters when they are particularly low and clear.

The compromises we've worked out vary a little. In the heavier waters of spring and early summer, I use a six-pound monofilament line and a four-pound leader the length of my rod. As soon as waters become sparkling clear and drop to summer levels, I switch to a four-pound line and two-pound leader. If I switch to spinning lures, I usually remove the leaders.

Dave and Ivor Evans, both perfectionists, lean to lighter leaders, although Dave now is experimenting again with a light fly line he can see better than monofilament. Neither ever uses anything heavier than a four-pound leader. Dave has even experimented with 7X tippets. He has landed many a heavy fish with extremely light tippets.

Using a two-pound line and 5X tippets, Dave gave me a bad shellacking one early June day on the East Koy. I was using a six-pound line and four-pound leader, and I was too stubborn or lazy to change. The drought that spring was severe. On that June day, the streams were lower than they usually are in mid-summer. I knew better but—. Anyway, at the end of the day, I didn't have a fish as large as Dave's smallest. I got little satisfaction from the fact that he estimated he lost "about a dozen" tackles while I had lost only six.

The following summer, there was a similar day on a weekend trip that Dave and I made to the Brodhead in Pennsylvania. I was using four-pound line and two-pound leader; Dave was using two-pound line and a 4X tip. Usually, over the season, Dave's catches and mine don't differ too much, but on this day the water again was extremely clear and low.

When I met him at noon, he had far better fish than I. He'd released a lot of fair fish. This time, I shifted fast. I had no line lighter than four pounds with me, but I doubled the length of my two-pound leader and also put on a 4X tip. Our afternoon catches were about equal.

chapter 7

Hooks to Choose
and Why

IN SELECTING HOOKS FOR WORMING, THERE ARE TWO important considerations apart from the obvious function of hooking the fish. One is the selection of a hook that will not be swallowed easily by small, especially under-sized, trout. The second is a hook rig that will permit you to slide your worm through bush and root tangles with as few hide-spoiling snag-ups as possible.

We've mentioned previously our strong preference for worm gangs. If you used singly the small No. 14 and No. 12 hooks that we tie up into gangs, you'd not only miss a lot of good fish but, more important, you'd kill a lot of small trout that would swallow such a small, single hook with ease. Gangs generally solve all the problems nicely.

In addition to the No. 14 and No. 12 hooks, I usually have a few gangs tied up with No. 16 hooks for very small worms. The hook point should stay inside the worm. When you keep the hook point buried, the trout will not feel it and, possibly, drop it like a hot potato. The fact that the hook point is inside the worm seems to have little effect on your ability to hook trout, providing you strike sharply.

There are several ways of tying gangs. With a wire-cutter, I snip off the eyes of the bottom hooks of the three-hook gangs I prefer. Each of these hooks, in turn, is placed in a fly-tying vise. A drop of clear fingernail lacquer is dropped onto the shank. The lacquer will nicely hold a piece of six-pound or four-pound monofilament until you can wrap it tightly to the shank with light silk or nylon thread. The lacquer also helps prevent the monofilament from pulling free from the shank when you may be playing a heavy fish. The thread should be heavily waxed to make it stick better.

The monofilament used to tie three-hook gangs should be about one and three-quarter inches and not more than two inches long. For two-hook gangs, it should be about one and one-half inches long. Use six-pound monofilament for No. 12 hooks, four-pound monofilament for No. 14 hooks and four-pound or two-pound monofilament for No. 16 hooks.

Remember that the hook size and monofilament thickness should depend more on the size of worms to be used than the size of the fish you hope to catch. Your objective is to use as light monofilament as possible, yet prevent balling of the worm.

After cutting the monofilament into short lengths, touch each end to a hot cigarette tip. The heat will cause a rough swelling at the ends and prevent them from slipping out of the threads under pressure.

Most gangs available commercially are too long. These evidently are intended for nightcrawlers. There is no disadvantage in using a short gang with a fairly long worm. In fact, the free, wiggling tail should be your objective,

Chemical Names and Formulae for "Freon" Refrigerants

Registered Trademark	Chemical Name	Formula	Boiling Point °F.
"F-11"	Trichloromonofluoromethane	CCl_3F	74.8°
"F-12"	Dichlorodifluoromethane	CCl_2F_2	−21.6°
"F-13"	Monochlorotrifluoromethane	$CClF_3$	−114.6°
"F-22"	Monochlorodifluoromethane	$CHClF_2$	−41.4°
"F-113"	Trichlorotrifluoroethane	$CCl_2F \cdot CClF_2$	117.6°
"F-114"	Dichlorotetrafluoroethane	$CClF_2 \cdot CClF_2$	38.4°
"F-502"	Azeotrope of "F-22" and "F-115"		−50.1°

ELECTRIC WIRE SIZE

MOTOR HP	SINGLE PHASE		THREE PHASE	
	115 Volt	230 Volt	230 Volt	460 Volt
⅓	14	14		
½	14	14	14	14
¾	12	14	14	14
1	12	14	14	14
1½	10	14	14	14
2		12	14	14
3		10	14	14
5			12	14
7½			10	14
10			8	12

From standards of The National Board of Fire Underwriters

Ton = 12,000 BTU per hour
Gal. Water = 8.33 lbs.
lb. = 7000 grains
Watt = 3.42 BTU per hour
Kilowatt = 1000 watts
H.P. = 746 watts
H.P. = 2545 BTU per hour

$C° = 5/9 \times (F° − 32°)$
$F° = 9/5 \times C° + 32°$
Foot Head = $2.31 \times$ lbs.

Motor Eff. = $\dfrac{HP \times 746 \times 100\%}{KW\ Input \times 1000}$

Pump Eff. % = $\dfrac{GPM \times 8.3 \times Ft.\ Hd.}{BHP \times 33,000}$

VAPOR PRESSURE, PSIG

Temp.	"F-11"	"F-12"	"F-502"	"F-22"	"F-113"	"F-114"	"F-13"	R-500*
−50	28.9	15.4	0.0	6.1		27.2	57.0	
−45	28.7	13.3	2.0	2.7		26.7		
−40	28.4	11.0	4.3	0.5		26.1	72.7	7.9
−35	28.1	8.4	6.7	2.5		25.5		4.8
−30	27.8	5.5	9.4	4.8	29.3	24.7	90.9	1.4
−25	27.4	2.3	12.3	7.3	29.2	23.9		1.1
−20	27.0	0.6	15.5	10.1	29.1	22.9	111.7	3.1
−15	26.5	2.4	19.0	13.1	28.9	21.8		5.4
−10	26.0	4.5	22.8	16.4	28.7	20.6	135.4	7.8
− 5	25.4	6.7	26.9	20.0	28.5	19.3		10.4
0	24.7	9.2	31.2	23.9	28.2	17.8	162.2	13.3
5	24.0	11.8	36.0	28.1	27.9	16.1		16.4
10	23.1	14.6	41.1	32.7	27.6	14.3	192.2	19.8
15	22.1	17.7	46.6	37.7	27.2	12.3		23.4
20	21.1	21.0	52.4	43.0	26.8	10.1	225.8	27.3
25	19.9	24.6	58.7	48.7	26.3	7.6		31.6
30	18.6	28.5	65.4	54.8	25.8	5.0	263.3	36.1
35	17.2	32.6	72.6	61.4	25.2	2.1		41.0
40	15.6	37.0	80.2	68.5	24.5	0.5	305.0	46.2
45	13.9	41.7	87.7	76.0	23.8	2.2		51.8
50	12.0	46.7	96.9	84.0	22.9	4.0	351.2	57.8
55	10.0	52.0	109.7	92.5	22.1	6.0		64.1
60	7.7	57.7	115.6	101.6	21.0	8.1	402.4	71.0
65	5.3	63.8	125.8	111.2	19.9	10.4		78.1
70	2.6	70.2	136.6	121.4	18.7	12.9	458.8	85.8
75	0.1	77.0	147.9	132.2	17.3	15.5	521.0	93.9
80	1.6	84.2	159.9	143.6	15.9	18.3		102.5
85	3.2	91.8	172.5	155.6	14.3	21.4		111.5
90	5.0	99.8	185.8	168.4	12.5	24.6		121.2
95	6.8	108.3	199.7	181.8	10.6	28.0		131.3
100	8.9	117.2	214.4	195.9	8.6	31.7		141.9
105	11.1	126.6	229.7	210.7	6.4	35.6		153.3
110	13.4	136.4	245.8	226.3	4.0	39.7		164.9
115	15.9	146.8	266.1	242.7	1.4	44.1		177.4
120	18.5	157.7	280.3	259.9	0.7	48.7		190.3
125	21.3	169.1	298.7	277.9	2.2	53.7		204.6
130	24.3	181.0	318.0	296.8	3.7	58.8		218.
135	27.4	193.5	338.1	316.5	5.4	64.3		233.
140	30.8	206.6	359.2	337.2	7.2	70.1		248.
145	34.4	220.3	381.1	358.8	9.2	76.3		
150	38.2	234.6	404.0	381.5	11.2	82.6		

Red Numerals = Inches Hg. Below 1 ATM
*Patented By Carrier Corporation

A-41370

even with small worms. The hooks are buried near the head of the worm.

You will want the eye, of course, on the top hook. Your leader will fasten directly to this eye. There should be no snell. A snell only creates a new carrying problem and adds a knot where you link the snell and leader. In my opinion, the two-hook gang is a compromise. You kill fewer fish with swallowed hooks than you will with a single hook and you hold your worm in a stretched out position. Furthermore, they require a little less time to tie. But you'll definitely kill more fish unintentionally than you will with a three-hook gang.

The gangs are carried in little glass bottles with screw caps, obtainable in drugstores. The bottles are only slightly longer than the gangs.

If you are caught on the stream with an insufficient number of gangs, you can use a single, short-shanked hook. For such emergencies I prefer the salmon-egg type of steelhead hook in No. 8 size. I always feel a little guilty when I use a single hook because I know that more fish, some unwanted or under legal size, will swallow it.

If an undersize fish does swallow it, I invariably cut the leader at the trout's mouth. In this way, I know that most of them will live, but some trout which have swallowed single hooks will be bleeding before you net them. These I keep, of course, unless they are undersized. You can minimize the killing of small fish by striking as soon as you feel a fish take the worm. Anyway, you get more fun from a lip-hooked fish.

It is a cause of great puzzlement to me why conservation departments, instead of setting a minimum limit on trout in all streams, don't require, instead, that trout anglers keep all trout they catch, regardless of size, up to their number limit. There would be more real conservation in such a law, in my opinion, than there is in a minimum limit. No real trout angler wants to take small trout. If he runs into many small trout, he is more likely to look for new water.

If anglers were required to take all trout landed, they'd be much more likely to move out of waters loaded with small fish. With the law as it stands, they can continue to catch, kill, and discard as carrion a great number of small fish while continuing along the stream in the hope of taking larger fish. Some anglers will do just that, deliberately, and without thought, apparently, of conservation.

Harry Coxon and I saw a horrible example of such waste and greed—plus poor timing by the New York State Conservation Department—on the Wiscoy one spring morning several years ago.

We started to fish a beautiful, wooded stretch a few miles below Pike one idyllic May morning, a day that quickly put bad tastes in our mouths. On a high bank along that stretch are several scattered summer cottages. We knew the owner of one of these cottages well and chatted with him before dropping down to the stream.

We liked the stretch particularly because it had not been stocked for several years. We like stretches like that. The remaining fish will be good ones and, because they are harder to catch than newly-stocked babies on other stretches, this type of water will have fewer anglers.

The cottager informed us that the stream had been stocked just a few days before. He and some of the game club boys from Pike had helped with the stocking. Somehow, the word got out and the tyros and once or twice-a-year trout fishermen flocked in.

It was sinful. The Conservation Department represented those fish as of legal size, seven inches. Actually, a high proportion of the fish were six and three-quarters and six and seven-eighths inches long. We measured them. We went down to the stream and walked along it for a few hundred yards. In every pool, we could see from two to a dozen dead trout lying on the bottom. There were broken gills protruding from the mouths of many of the fish.

Here was sheer, savage waste. The greenhorns undoubtedly would have been glad to prevent that waste by keeping the trout. If they did prevent the waste and keep the trout, a game warden would see to it that they were punished.

If the trout had been kept in the fish hatchery a few weeks longer, they would have been full legal size. The sportsman's money, which keeps the hatcheries going, would not have been wasted. Why did the Conservation Department choose that period in spring, when fishing pressure was heaviest, to dump just-undersize fish on such a well-known and heavily fished stream?

If they had to be dumped for some good reason, why weren't they placed in a less heavily fished stream, or preferably, in some good feeder where they might have a chance to grow up?

Other anglers learned about the wasteful carnage. There were hot letters to the Conservation Department but never a satisfactory answer. We wonder if the elimination of a minimum size wouldn't help prevent such waste again. The Province of Ontario now requires that all black bass taken, regardless of size, be retained.

For the first few years at least, Ontario has had good results with the new law. Serious anglers just do not want to make a point of catching small fish. If they find an area loaded with small fish, they'll get out so they are not forced to take them. If they do injure a small fish, they keep it. Their only punishment is in their regret that the small fish may prevent them from taking a larger one. In any event, they are not forced to drop the fish back into the water to rot.

One suggestion remains on the use of a single hook when worm fishing for trout. The hook always must be placed near the head of the worm. Hooking the worm in the tougher collar is good practice. Better yet, insert the point of the hook at the head of the worm and run it around the curve of the hook. Leave the hook point inside the worm.

chapter 8

Sinkers

EXCELLENT COIL SINKERS MAY BE PURCHASED FROM L. L. Bean of Freeport, Maine. They come in a convenient paper-match type of package and you need no separate container to hold them. They are of ideal thickness and length for most any condition you will encounter.

Dave and Ivor Evans, who can't be surpassed as top-notch trout anglers, still go through the early spring ritual of making their own sinkers from sheet lead, and tying their worm gangs. I also tie worm gangs but use the lead-cutting time to tie dry flies and, sometimes, a superoo wet fly that I hope will lure an Atlantic salmon the next time I get to the Miramichi.

The Evans brothers have regular plumbers' sheet lead rolled to about twenty or twenty-two-thousandths of an inch thickness, in a metal-working shop, then cut the lead with a shears to the width and length they desire.

Their leads are from one-sixteenth to three-thirty-seconds of an inch wide and range to about five inches

long. They coil these leads in advance around a fine wire
and carry the coils in tall glass or plastic bottles.

The Evans brothers like their sinkers a foot or more
from the hook. I prefer a sinker closer to the hook. So do
Ockie Swanson, Irv Conrad, and a few other good wormers.

There is good sense in the reasoning of the Evans boys.
They figure that when the sinker is farther from the hook,
the worm has freer and more natural movement in floating
downstream. They are right in this. Furthermore, they
regard the sinker as somewhat of a warning to a trout. I
differ with them in that respect. Actually, I regard the
sinker as more of an attraction than not. When it is closer
to the hook, it is a little easier to place your worm accurately, especially in a wind. The Evans brothers' method
of fastening the coils to a leader is simple. The wire on
which they form the coils leaves a hole. They merely push
the monofilament through the hole, then twist and stretch
out the lead around the monofilament so smoothly that
you can hardly see it at a distance.

I prefer the L. L. Bean strips, which are about 30-
thousandths of an inch thick, about ³⁄₃₂nds of an inch wide,
⅛th inch wide and 1½ inches long. They tear out of the
paper-match-type cover easily. You wrap them on by
starting the wrap in the middle of the lead strip. Make
sure the ends are pinched down neatly. A smooth sinker,
without even small projections, will ride through many
snags.

We've never found any make of lead strip in sporting
goods stores that wasn't too thin or too wide. With such
strips, your sinker either will be too light or too bulky.
You'll gain nothing over regular split shot in using such
strips. In fact, if I had no alternative, I'd prefer the split

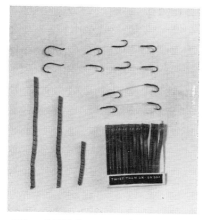

The skillful wormer's terminal tackle. The single hooks are #8s; the hooks on the gangs are #14s. Varying lead lengths permit quick changes of weight for different stream conditions.

The proper position for fishing good trout hides.

A low approach is vital for fishing smooth pools.

Roll-casting a worm works well on certain stretches.

Ivor Evans floats a small worm down a promising run, keeping his rod tip downstream from the worm to avoid drag.

Reaching in far underneath overhanging trees often pays off.

The quiet pockets on the far side of fast water should get close attention.

Even if the water is shallow, the deep shade under bridges attracts many trout.

Fishing shallow hides can be profitable.

A creelful of fish will make any angler happy.

A wormer nets a good one on Deckertown Creek in central New York.

The author with a big one.

Bob Bromnick, well-known upstream spinner, holds a ten-pound, eight-ounce brown taken from the Credit River in Ontario.

A wormer tries a pretty spot on western New York's Wiscoy.

The upstream spinner can cover a whole series of trout hides in one cast.

A spin caster leans far forward to work his lure near the brushy bank.

Bucky Sieminski, skilled upstream spinner, slides his net under a nice brownie.

An upstream spinner approaches a quiet pool through the protective cover of riffles.

shot, hanging from a separate monofilament dropper about three inches long, extending from the leader at a point about ten or twelves inches above the worm. The dropper permits you to add and remove shot easily. This arrangement, however, will mean more snags.

chapter 9

Scouring and Carrying Worms

SMALL BLACKHEAD WORMS, THE TYPE YOU DIG OUT OF clay loam, are a treasure to the skilled wormer. They are naturally tough and, even though you don't like your steak that way, trout love them. From the same type of soil you also get "pinkies," a smaller, more-delicate worm but equally well-liked by trout. Red worms of the type you get from richer soil and leaf piles are satisfactory if the other two types are not available, but they usually are soft and tear off the hook or hooks easily. Avoid like poison those smelly manure worms with barred yellow and red bodies. Trout do not like them.

Alec Henderson invariably scoured his worms. Our gang usually does too, but sometimes we are too lazy or don't have time. Scouring definitely toughens the worms and makes them more lively. A lively worm is essential to good fishing results. If any worm on our hooks doesn't give good action or is torn slightly by a snag or chub, we replace it immediately.

Scoured worms hold up well. Sometimes I suspect they may be more delectable to the trout. From the viewpoint of fine flavor, however, I think at other times that a worm directly from the ground is just as acceptable. Old Alec always contended that a nightcrawler tastes bitter to a trout. I don't know how he knew. I never tried one.

I do know that, fished by equally-good fishermen, a dug worm will take far more trout than a nightcrawler at any time except, possibly, during the cold-water fishing of early spring. Our gang tested all types of worms and we're all thoroughly sold on the foregoing conclusion.

Probably the easiest method of scouring worms is to place blackheads or pinkies in a closely-jointed box filled with damp sphagnum moss. Feed them every few days with applications of ground cornmeal. Check on your worms to make sure all are alive. Make sure to remove any dead ones. In a week, your worms will be almost transparent. They'll be a little smaller, but they'll be fighting mad. Scoured worms definitely are to be recommended.

After a few weeks, the moss will become smelly. Then remove all worms and wash the moss thoroughly in cold water before replacing it, and the worms, in the box.

Most store-purchased worm boxes are made of metal or plastic. Such boxes are entirely unsatisfactory, because of the heat and cold they conduct so rapidly. In lieu of something better, Dave Evans used to carry worms in a canvas bag pinned to his coat. The bag had a draw string. It was filled with sphagnum moss. I noted that Dave's worms kept lively in the hottest of weather but they chilled quickly in cold weather. Also, Dave frequently became obviously impatient when he tried to fish a worm out of the bag.

Most of our gang now strongly favors wooden boxes. They are light, have fine insulating qualities, and the unpainted interiors seems to agree with the worms. We never did succeed in making a satisfactory box with joints. No matter how we did it, no matter what glue we used, in a short time the necessary dampness in the box always caused warping. We even tried laminated boxes but they, too, did not stand the test of time. Without doubt, the best box is drilled and gouged out of a solid block of well-seasoned but not aromatic wood. You can't buy such a box in a sporting goods store. You have to make it or have it made.

Clear white pine works well. Cedar and redwood, despite their resistance to rot, don't seem to agree so well with the worms. I've often thought I'd like to try cypress but I've never succeeded in getting a block sufficiently large. The outside dimensions of my present box are six by four inches. The walls and bottom are about a halfinch thick. The box is curved slightly to conform with the curve of my waist. Two narrow pieces of aluminum are offset at the rear of the box to permit passage of a trousers belt. A piece of well-painted marine plywood, one-fourth-inch thick, is hinged to the box as a cover.

chapter 10

How to Cast a Worm

IN OUR EARLY DAYS OF LEARNING THE TECHNIQUES OF ALEC Henderson, all of us practiced precision in the placing of a worm. Neighbors sometimes looked askance at Dave Evans and me, among others, when we'd hie off to the back lawn on warmer days during the winter and cast fully rigged rods and lines to small rock-targets and under kitchen chairs. The chairs, of course, were the equivalent of an overhanging bush. To simulate the weight of a worm, we'd tie on pieces of wet absorbent cotton. Sometimes the cotton would freeze while we were using it.

The bread-and-butter cast is strictly underhand. You use little more line than the length of your rod. If you want to cast farther, coil some line in your hand and shoot it through the guides. Not that you want to do so very often but it is simple to cast a worm thirty or forty feet in this way. Much more important than distance is accuracy. You should be able to place a worm consistently within inches of where you want it, even in a wind. Inches often mean the difference between fish and no fish. Don't be satisfied with placing your bait ALMOST where you want it. Strive for pinpoint accuracy. The time you spend practicing will pay off. You want to get right in close to hides or right into them, even though you may lose tackle. You do not want to be a foot, or even six inches, away.

While we've emphasized the desirability of a short line, there are a very few skilled wormers who can use a medium-length line consistently with deadly results. By medium length, let's say a line twice or triple the length of the rod.

There's no doubt that, properly handled, the medium-length line will take many trout. It minimizes the problem of stream approach. You take fewer chances of the fish seeing you, of them being disturbed by noise and vibrations.

The rub in this method is that it is much more difficult to make precision casts. Only a few wormers with long experience can cast right on the button with a medium-length line. In addition, the medium-line wormer has more problems in avoiding line drag although it is possible to do so with lightweight monofilament, on which rushing water exerts far less pressure than on a conventional fly line.

In situations calling for a medium-length line, I usually strip off and hold in my left hand the amount of line I intend to shoot. To get better rod leverage, I usually point the rod tip at about a forty-five-degree angle to the left of the body and swing the worm and sinker upstream with a decisive flip. This cast, of course, is good only when fishing a left-handed bank while facing upstream. When fishing a right-handed bank, the rod should start at an angle to the right of the body. The trick is stopping the shooting line at just the proper point to place the worm where you want it. No instructions will help you here. It requires practice, often years of it, unless you are one of those rare individuals who learn almost everything with a few trys.

Ivor Evans developed a medium-length cast that is superb, both for accuracy and delicacy. He points his rod directly at the target, letting only five or six feet of line dangle from the tip. Then he swings this line underhanded several times in the direction of the target, the rod tip held at about an eleven o'clock position in front of him. On the delivery, he lowers the rod tip to around half-past nine and flicks it upward and outward. On the delivery, his rod tip never goes higher than half-past ten; yet he can shoot his line straight ahead as far as thirty or forty feet. Usually he doesn't try for quite that distance. His average cast probably will be between twenty-two and twenty-eight feet. He strips in line by coiling it in his hand, as so many dry-fly men do.

The danger in his type of cast is that unless his timing is perfect, the worm will tend to go high into the air, possibly catching on an overhanging limb. But a high cast seldom happens with Ivor. In fact, he is consistently able to shoot a worm under low bushes. I like the cast very much, but haven't mastered it. When I need a medium-length line in a tight spot calling for extreme accuracy, I still lob the worm in with a partial side cast, using only enough power to shoot as much line as needed. I strip in line by hooking it under the index finger of my right hand and drawing big coils around the finger tip. The big coils are less likely to jam in the guides when you shoot line on the next cast. Incidentally, make a point of immediately reeling up any line you do not intend to use on the next cast. Excess line in your hand often can be a source of trouble.

In any worming cast, short, medium or long, don't

start your cast with any longer line than the length of your rod. You get much more leverage, much better control, with the shorter line. If the line with which you start your cast is much longer than your rod, you will not be able to utilize the rod's spring to flick it out.

chapter 11

Best Worming Streams

THE WORMING METHODS SUGGESTED IN THIS BOOK APPLY primarily to brown trout on heavily fished Eastern streams, particularly those that do not have enough insect life to keep brownies well-fed.

Such streams are numerous and there are times on normal fly streams when a worm will provide action and pleasure while flies will do little.

There are many streams, both large and small, in Vermont, New Hampshire, Massachusetts, New Jersey, Pennsylvania, North Carolina, Tennessee, and Michigan that have produced nice brownies for our gang of wormers. The gin-clear Peabody River of New Hampshire has been good to me on several occasions in short stopovers while on the way to or from New Brunswick's Atlantic salmon waters. So have Pine Creek, Kettle Creek, and the Brodhead in Pennsylvania, the gushing streams flowing out of the Great Smokies, the sandy headwaters of the Manistee River in Michigan, and many others.

I can't recommend worms for Western Loch Levens

(brown trout) although I'm sure the Loch Levens would be an easy mark at many times of the year. In fact, I've seen some Salt Lake City wormers take nice Loch Levens during June on the lower Madison River. On Western streams, generally, you can get enough action with a dry fly to satisfy yourself completely. I'll always prefer a fly if I can get action with it.

I must confess to the use of a worm one afternoon on Montana's intriguing Big Hole River. Fly fishermen, including myself, had done little for days during an unusually hot spell late in September. Even such a superb fly man as Joe Brooks left the Big Hole during that period to seek greener pastures, but he returned about a week later with Dan Bailey, the former university professor who gave up teaching to become the leading trout-tackle manufacturer in the Yellowstone area and probably the best-informed angler in that section. They took trout on flies after they returned, but during the hot period the Big Hole seemed dead. As a last resort, I turned to my two aces in the hole—worms and upstream spinning.

Just upstream from the village of Twin Bridges, Montana the Big Hole divides around a sizable island. On one side of the island the stream is big and powerful. The branch on the other side is small, brushy, filled with logs, hard to fish. Many local anglers, particularly the enthusiasts who abound in Butte, seemed able to find time each day to fish. They pounded the main branch. In keeping with my policy of looking for second-best places when a stream is being pounded, I swung up the small branch one of those hot days, with the dry air so exhilaratingly clear that I could plainly see snow-capped mountains fifty to seventy miles away. As usual, I looked for boot tracks in the sandy patches on both sides of the stream to determine whether I had competition. There were none. I had the small branch to myself. It looked fishy. It was, but the trout did not respond to dry flies so—

Within two hours, I had a heavy creel. I kept nothing under sixteen inches. I lost much tackle and several dandy fish under brush and logs, but I was happy. Both worms and spinning lures had worked well. I tried the lures after I had kept several good fish hooked on worms.

I never reached the head of the island. I stopped at a point where beavers had constructed a pond. When I dropped downstream to the main river, other anglers checked with me and asked where the fish had been taken, what I had been using. I told them freely about the worms and spinning lures but gestured only vaguely in the direction of the island in response to questions about the stretch I'd fished. The second-best branch produced well for me in subsequent days. When I left, I told Dan Bailey about it. I'm sure it produced for him too.

chapter 12

When to Fish

A HIGH PROPORTION OF TROUT ANGLERS WISELY START fishing early in the morning. Many of these either will quit before noon or take it easy from around noon until the sun's shadows start to lengthen in the late afternoon. On most streams and most days, that is good practice for a fly fisherman. Sometimes it is good practice for the wormer, too, but often the slack period for the fly fisherman becomes an excellent period for the wormer.

I've stopped trying to beat the horde to good water. It just can't be done. When a mob is thrashing through and along a stream, even hides that they do not fish often are disturbed. You'll often see anglers wading noisily right down the middle of smaller streams without even bothering to think of the next guy.

At that time of the year, I've stopped setting the alarm clock. I don't even try to get to a stream before ten or eleven o'clock. By then, the crowd usually has thinned out greatly and the stream has had a chance to settle down. Cold early-morning water has had a chance to warm up.

Starting late in the morning with a worm, it is surprising how many good trout may be taken from second-best hides. I've netted many a limit in these hours, releasing most of them. I've frequently felt I had a fine day and left the stream before the choice evening hours. This is the time of the season, however, when you must concentrate —more than at any other time—on fishing the second-best places that many anglers skip.

During the hot summer months, of course, the early-morning hours will almost always produce the best browns. It is a well-known fact that big browns feed primarily in the hours of darkness. In the morning hours, before the sun's rays chase the big fish back under their hides, you often can catch them in shallow riffles that lead into pools. Almost always, a hide will be near.

Early-morning fishing on the less crowded streams of summer also gives you other advantages. The water temperature then is usually at its lowest. Just as the cold waters of early spring mornings will tend to make a brown trout inactive, so will warm water in a hot summer period.

Another early-morning advantage is the opportunity to be the first man fishing a stretch on that day. Those opportunities usually increase through the summer as anglers turn to bass, perch, and pike. When you have first crack at a stream, you often can fish to advantage all the obvious pools that later in the day may be pounded to death.

Except for early-morning fishing in such hot-weather periods, it is wise to concentrate your efforts on sections of a stream where there are spring holes or where cool brooks flow into the main stream. Here, an intimate knowledge of a stream helps greatly.

Anglers fishing a stream in mid-summer almost invariably are confirmed trout men and they too will be concentrating on obvious brooks and spring holes. If you have

wisely spotted less obvious springs and brooks on earlier
fishing trips, you'll find your knowledge often is extremely
rewarding. Trout will concentrate around such spots,
sometimes so heavily that catching them ceases to be fun.

There is one spot along a certain stream in Western
New York that has seldom failed me in a hot period. It is
on a major stream but in a section of that stream that is
seldom stocked. You work hard for every fish you take.
The fish you do take usually are heavy. Few anglers
bother to try it. When they do, chubs will drown their
dry flies or devour their worms almost as fast as they can
cast them.

The stretch runs through a little hamlet. I've observed
that many anglers will avoid fishing in villages, partly, I
believe, because houses suggest crowds and heavy fishing
pressure, partly because of the psychological displeasure
that you get from angling in someone's backyard. I don't
like the latter, either, but I've found many fine fish right
in the heart of some villages. To partly offset the backyard
psychology, I often have such stretches all to myself on
days in which more-isolated stretches are crowded with
other anglers. Almost always, you'll find more anglers and
more hunters parked along isolated, dirt roads, if such
roads lead to fish and game territory, than you'll find along
main roads. You'll seldom see them working in or around
villages.

The hot-weather spot I like so well is hard to detect.
I spotted it first one sizzling Independence Day. The temperature had been in the nineties for several days. Frank
Cramer and I started fishing at dawn. We took some fair
fish and Frank lost a beauty. By noon we were wringing
wet from perspiration. We started walking back to the
car together. After lunch, we'd head for a stretch on the

East Koy, where we knew of several cold brooks in a little fished stretch.

At one point, high, densely wooded banks on both sides of the stream forced us into the stream itself. On top of one of the banks were two homes. We were apparently the only anglers on the stretch that day and we waded carelessly through the water on the shallow side of the stream. On the deep side was a magnificent, brush-covered hole in which I had lost two tackles before landing a twelve-inch brownie shortly after dawn. We were in water only about two inches deep when a whopper brown scooted off in front of me, its dorsal fin sticking up plainly as it knifed through the shallows. Several other large but lesser fish also raced away. All of the fish swung into the deep pool.

When we had it pointed out to us by the fish, Frank and I could see why those trout were lying in the shallows. From an impenetrable clump of alders flowed a spring. I dug for a stream thermometer in my fishing vest and tested the water. The temperature of the water where the trout had been lying was sixty-five degrees. The temperature of the water in the main stream was a shocking seventy-eight degrees. We marked the spring, of course, but there was little use in fishing that spot the rest of that day in view of the scare we had thrown into those browns.

I had to work the next day but Frank took off for that spring hole alone. It was another hot day. Frank invited no one. This was a spot we didn't plan to talk about. Frank drove up that evening as I was sitting on the front porch of my home. Inside an ice cooler, he had the big fish we'd spotted the day before. It weighed four and one-half pounds. He had two other fish about two pounds each.

Along about noon, he'd sneaked up carefully to that

spring hole and, considering the shallowness of the water in which he figured the trout would be lying, removed the sinker on his line. He knelt as he cast a long line, quartering upstream so the line wouldn't pass over the fish first. The big trout took the worm on the second cast.

Frank must have had a helluva time keeping the fish from burying itself among the many obstructions in the deep hole near the spring, but here it was, in the cooler. He caught one of his two-pounders from below a spring hole on another stream, then returned to the original hole late in the afternoon to take the other two-pounder. He had released a half-dozen smaller fish taken during the day.

From that spring hole Frank and I have taken dozens of beautiful trout on hot summer days in the years since. We've never seen another angler fish it during the summer. We've told only one other member of our gang about it. He takes fish there, too. If we told the rest of the boys —well, they have their little secrets, too.

Trout do tend to concentrate in cool-water areas during hot weather. There they have a place where they can be reasonably comfortable and where eating is probably less of a problem than keeping cool. Sometimes you will find it extremely difficult, if not impossible, to take even spring-hole trout.

Some experiences come to mind that illustrate this. There was the isolated spring hole on the Riviere Blanche (White River) in Quebec. I'd been having fine success with one- to three-pound brook trout, using brightly-colored wet flies. They were gorgeous specimens.

I learned from a friendly native that the first thing you had to do to catch the brookies in this stream was to excite them. For a man who concentrates on brown trout, deliberately exciting a trout seems ridiculous. But that's the way it worked on the Riviere Blanche. You'd cast into a pool or deep run carelessly. You'd make a point of lifting the line out of the water sharply, deliberately creating a splash. Your first trout usually would be small and you'd help that trout make all the commotion possible, playing the fish out to the limit. From then on, trout would come easier and easier and larger and larger. It was a queer method but it worked.

Then a hot spell developed. The friendly native told us about an isolated spring hole, about two miles upstream from a certain bridge. My wife and I found no path. We just plunged through the dense brush so typical of Quebec. We weren't disappointed. We came to a deep, cold brook.

Where the brook entered the main stream was a patch of tall grass. The patch was only as large as an average living room but it would provide an opportunity to cast. I sneaked through the grass and peered into the pool which the brook had created.

I remember how hard my heart thumped in the moments after that look. The pool was literally teeming with brook trout ranging up to three and four pounds. I shook so hard that I stuck the point of a hook into my finger twice before I succeeded in tying on two flies.

I sneaked again to a casting position, still partly concealed in the high grass. The water was so clear that, after I cast, I could easily see one of the flies settle on the nose of a lunker, then slip off. The trout merely moved to the side a little, gently fanning its white fins.

Scores of other big trout were lined up on both sides of this trout, all facing the cold water of the brook, all motionless except for the gentle movements of their fins. Not a trout moved an inch for my flies. I changed patterns. That made no difference. Then I changed to a spinner. Still nothing happened. I dragged out the can of worms that a farm boy had dug for me and rigged up light equipment. The worms didn't yield a strike, either, even though I placed them right at the nose of many fish. It was maddening.

That night I tossed in bed, trying to figure out some solution. No answer came to me but the next day, while hot, was slightly cooler than the previous day. My wife decided against the hard trek through the brush and I went alone. I started early to take advantage of the rela-tively-cooler morning temperature.

When I peered through the grass that morning, I could see the trout moving around. They had abandoned their stacked-cordwood positions, temporarily at least. In an hour, I took three beauties on a Dark Montreal. Then, as the heat grew, the number of fish near the brook grew and I could get no more strikes on flies. I tried worms for awhile and took another. A spinner yielded a fifth fish. By that time, the heat again was almost stifling and the trout were lined up like cordwood. That was all for that day. It turned cold after a thunderstorm that afternoon. At the mouth of the brook the next morning, there wasn't a trout in sight.

Frank Avery, Joe Rigler, and I had an amusing experi-ence with spring-hole trout on the North Branch of the Saranac River years ago. We had read in an outdoor magazine about the superb fishing some writer had found on a stream north of Saranac Lake Village. The writer had made sure not to pinpoint the stream but he had given enough clues so that, with the aid of a U.S. topographical map, we thought we could find this super-duper stretch. Whether we found his stretch or not, we sure found something just as good.

To reach the spot, we had to drive over some roads that were little more than cowpaths. They've been improved in the years since, but at that time the brush at each side

of the road scratched the side of the car, even snapped
into our faces through the open windows. Our transmis-
sion hit bottom several times. That was in the days when
autos had road clearances of nine and ten inches, not the
present damnable five and six. At one point, we had to
cross a rickety bridge over a brook. The roadbed of that
bridge consisted solely of two unfastened two-by-twelve
planks. Some other vehicle had bounced the planks out
of position so we got out and straightened them. Underneath the planks were several cross members, space, and
water. We crossed the bridge and continued on a few
miles to still another bridge with a similar plank arrangement.

This brook was much wider. A few feet downstream
from the bridge, the brook entered into the North Fork.
As he started to straighten the planks, Joe spotted fish
under the bridge. We looked more closely. Holy smoke,
they were trout, whopper trout, bunched up apparently
to escape the warmer waters of the North Fork, which is
a fairly-cold stream in itself. It had been frightfully hot
for weeks.

We had brought with us from our camp at Wilmington
Notch a likeable and enthusiastic young fellow who was
honeymooning in a tent at the campsite. He'd seen us
come into camp with some catches of trout and was eager
to learn. He was even willing to abandon his bride for a
day.

For fishing equipment, he had the usual conglomeration
that many amateurs carry, a short, inexpensive bass-casting
rod, a cheap reel and line, and a tackle box containing a
few hooks, sinkers and nondescript plugs and a bass bug.

Without realizing it until later, that boy really gave us
an angling lesson that day. We couldn't assemble our tackle
fast enough to get at those spring-hole fish. Meanwhile,

we discussed how we could fish for them most effectively
without disturbing them.

The water under the bridge was fast but very clear.
It probably was about three feet deep in the area where
the trout were concentrated. The stream is about twenty
feet wide at that point. We broke through the brush on
both sides of the stream, well back from the bank so the
trout couldn't see us. The newlywed, who also was a
gentleman, decided not to "spoil your chances" and elected
to watch from a position on the road near the bridge.

Frank, Joe, and I worked our hearts out for hours without a sign of interest on the part of the trout. We used
dry and wet flies, streamers, spinners, and worms. We
caught minnows, grasshoppers, and frogs and used them
too, also unsuccessfully. We had lunch and decided to ex-
plore further up the brook. The newlywed decided to
fish off the bridge. It was almost dark before we quit. We
had succeeded in landing only a few small trout.

We started back for camp. Naturally, all we talked
about was those big trout under the bridge and what we
could do on some cooler day to take them.

"You know, it was funny," interjected the newlywed,
whose name I can't recall. "When you fellows went upstream, I tried worms for awhile. I hung a worm right in
front of the noses of those fish and they didn't budge.
Then I thought I'd try one of the bass bugs in my tackle
box. Funny, but for about a half-hour a trout would come
up and grab one of those bugs nearly every time I dropped
it in the water. But the darned fish would take the bug
to the bottom and then let go. I couldn't figure out what
was the matter with them."

I'll never forget that experience. As I recall it, Joe
slammed on his brakes in the darkness. We stared at the

newlywed. He was telling the truth, all right. He was just too green to realize the opportunity he'd had. We moaned and demanded to see the bug he had been using. It was still on his rod, the hook around one of the cross members of his reel.

Dark or not, we drove many miles that night, looking for a store that might still be open and might have bugs similar to the one used by the newlywed. We found one. All of us were fishing that brook at dawn the next morning. We fished in the area all that day. We bass-bugged the brook for a mile or more. Those bugs never did work again, so far as our party was concerned, but we did catch a wonderful mess on worms several days later, when the weather cooled.

The following description of an experience at a spring hole might help you take trout when they seem to be unable to decide whether they are more concerned with the heat or their appetites. Frank Avery and I were fishing the Ausable near the village of Black Brook. For the Adirondacks, the heat had been terrific, in the nineties almost every day. In the cool hours of morning that day, we caught several fish. Frank's wet flies were far more effective than my drys. Then, near noon, we couldn't move a fish. I worked upstream to a certain deep bay, which I knew was watered at its far end by a gushing brook. Where the bay entered the main stream, I took the water temperature and found it about five degrees cooler than in a nearby riffle of the river.

As I worked into the narrow bay with a dry fly, I started to spot trout. Actually, most of the trout spotted me first. I saw several good ones dart away. I decided to move no more. I eased over to a low, gravel bar at the side of the bay and gave the trout a chance to get over their

scare. I figured there must be trout in the bay that hadn't
seen me. I sat there contentedly for about a half-hour in
the shade of a big sycamore tree before trying again.

From my post under the tree I started to cast again,
getting down on my knees. I speculated all over that pool
with my dry fly, changing patterns several times. Nothing
happened. The water in the bay had practically no movement so I tried twitching the fly. That didn't help either.
I tried a wet fly without success, then started to fix up a
worm rig. Somehow, there is a comforting feeling to have
that ace in the hole, even though you don't expect to use
it. On brown trout, at least, it usually will work when
everything else fails.

The water in that bay probably averaged two feet deep.
The bottom was strewn with head-size granite rocks. I
used a very small sinker to carry the worm to the bottom.
A trout quickly picked up the worm, then dropped it. I
replaced the worm and cast again.

I cussed my awkwardness with the relatively short dry-
fly rod I had with me. The worm splashed, much more
than I like, and I saw a fish race away from it. I cast more
carefully to another part of the bay. Again, a trout picked
up the worm and dropped it.

Then I wised up. Here I was doing little more than
dunking. For practical purposes there was no current in
the water. The worm couldn't drift. All it could do was
go straight to the bottom. It was doing even that unnaturally. My sinker, light as it was, was carrying it down
far more rapidly than it would sink if it had just fallen
into the water from a bank. When the trout had picked
up the worm, they probably were already suspicious.
When they felt the slight weight of the sinker, they became convinced.

I removed the sinker. I was using the same 4X tippet

that I had been using with the dry fly. I cast again and saw the worm sink much more slowly, much more naturally toward the bottom. A trout had it before it reached the bottom. Without moving from my knees, I slid a nice sixteen-incher onto the gravel bar about five minutes later.

I smoked a cigarette while I waited for the pool to quiet down and cast again. Another trout took the worm before it reached bottom. When Frank came up to me a while later, I was still in the shade of the sycamore. I had quit fishing. I had all the trout I wanted. Every one of my unweighted worms was taken before it hit the bottom. This seems to contradict my earlier emphasis on keeping the worm on the bottom, but fishing in that bay presented an exceptional situation, not typical of day-in and day-out trout fishing on a stream with moving water.

chapter 13

How to Spot
Trout Hides

Always look for any obstruction that permits water to run beneath it. Don't worry about the depth so long as the water will cover a trout's back. Close observation and concentration is required to spot such places, the kind of places you formerly may have passed up. But trout may be found in any pocket of that kind. Hard-to-fish spots of that type are the places on which to concentrate on a heavily fished stream.

When you encounter many fishermen, or know that others are ahead, watch the stream constantly with the thought uppermost in your mind of spotting the places other anglers are not likely to fish. When you come to a beautiful pool of the type that no one skips, study it carefully, both upstream and down, for hard-to-reach pockets that other anglers may pass up.

Look particularly for possible hides along the far bank

just above the point where riffles or rapids enter a pool.

There's something in human nature that makes people look for the best they can get. That applies to anglers too. Most trout men will concentrate on the best-looking portion of a pool, then move on to the next pool. On a heavily fished stream, these are poor tactics. Instead, look for the second-best and third-best portions of that pool and concentrate on those spots. At first, you'll find that you have to force yourself to look for the second-best spots. Like the other anglers, your eye will be drawn to what seems to be the best. Don't let your eye wander. Second best often is best.

I recall a Sunday in May on Oatka Creek, near Rochester, New York, when Dave Evans proved that point very conclusively. The stream was loaded with Rochester anglers. On several beautiful pools, near which we parked our car, as many as seven or eight fishermen lined the bank. There seemed to be fewer anglers in the less attractive water downstream and we cruised along the bank, sizing up prospects in the channels between the water weeds that are so prevalent in that stream.

Dave walked into the stream first and I marked the spot. I'd walk farther downstream and fish up but I wouldn't fish over the water Dave had covered. I'd be wasting my time.

It was a sultry day and rain threatened, but the gay mating calls of meadowlarks, killdeer, and robins filled the air. Leaves on the maples and willows bordering the stream were that refreshing light green that they have at no other time of the year. At the side of the stream was a cherry orchard, the soft pink blossoms waving gently in a light breeze. Sultry and all, it was a good day to be alive.

Both Dave and I had fair fish when I caught up with

him just downstream from the first big pool. The stream was wide at that point, possibly two hundred feet, but most of that water was shallow and the rocks slippery.

I saw Dave studying the pool. When I came up to him, he informed me flatly that he was going to take a trout from "under those guys' noses."

We checked later and found only a few small fish among all of the worm dunkers circling that pool.

Running into the pool was a shallow riffle that didn't average more than a few inches deep. A few feet above the point where the riffle slid into the deeper water of the pool, a large bush was lying in the water, only a few of its roots still clinging to the eroded bank. It dangled downstream along the bank, its branches quivering in the gentle current.

The bank at the point where the bush dragged in the water was about two feet high. Anglers crossing the stream to reach the other side of the pool undoubtedly had crossed about twenty-five feet upstream, where the bank became a gravel bar. We could see the boot prints going up the bar. Between the bush and the pool, a barbed wire fence crossed the stream.

I waded over to the bush with Dave. I saw what he meant. Under the bush was a dark little pocket, possibly ten inches deep. There was a good chance of snagging up but so what?

Dave pulled off a section of sinker from his leader and took a new one out of a bottle. He jockeyed carefully into position and cast. I could see the worm disappear under the bush a few feet upstream from the pocket. Then his line started to throb and Dave struck. He strikes as soon as he feels a fish. Most of the rest of our gang wait a second or two. His powerful strike drew out from under that bush a beautiful brown.

It leaped high into the air almost immediately, then plunged abruptly downstream into the pool, where another leap close to the shore caused a startled worm dunker to take a backward step from his position near the bank.

"Fish on," I yelled, and the anglers considerately reeled up their lines.

It was a pretty job of fish handling in an unglamorous place. Dave held his rod low when the fish started down into the pool so the line wouldn't scrape along the barbed wire fence. From this position, he fought the fish until the frenzy of its rushes had died down. Then he waded over to the fence and passed the rod under the bottom strand, reaching over the fence with his other hand to grab the butt. From then on, Dave played the trout over the top of the fence. I crawled over the fence and a few minutes later netted a fish weighing just under four pounds.

We moved on to see if the next crowded pool might have similar possibilities. After we had waded a way upstream, we looked back and grinned. Four of the dunkers had lines under the bush from which Dave had taken his fish.

The second-best hide on the next pool proved unproductive, but Dave took a fourteen-incher from under a weed clump at the tail of the third pool. He had an audience to watch him land that fish, too. The water was no more than six inches deep.

In looking for trout hides, always keep in mind the tendency of trout to lie in relatively quiet water at the edge of a fast current. When a hide is in quieter water at the edge of fast water, you can almost count on it to hold fish.

In floating your worm down through a pool or deep run, concentrate on the very edge of the fast water, where it seems to slice through a quieter portion of the pool or run.

If that quieter portion is toward the other side of the stream, make sure you hold your rod tip high enough so that the line angle is as near the perpendicular as possible. This will tend to prevent the fast water from sweeping the worm downstream too rapidly. Little things like that often mean the difference between a fish and no fish.

In addition to bushes, trees, logs, overhanging rocks, and undercut banks, there is one type of hide that almost always merits attention, even though there may be no hide at all in the stream itself. That is a bridge. The shade provided by a bridge has a powerful attraction for trout.

Furthermore, low bridges often are extremely difficult to fish properly because of the problem of placing accurate casts under them sufficiently far upstream to reach all the fish that may be lurking there. Never pass up a low-lying bridge, regardless of the type of water flowing under it. Under a bridge, even shallow riffles may produce. If it is impossible to fish under the bridge from a downstream position, float a worm under it from an upstream position, throwing enough slack line to permit good coverage. Once you pull your worm unnaturally upstream from under that bridge, however, you can figure you've probably ruined your chances.

chapter 14

Floating the Worm

WHEN YOU FEEL YOUR SINKER STRIKE BOTTOM SEVERAL feet upstream from the suspected hide of a trout, you must be on the alert to prevent the worm from staying in one spot at the bottom of the stream for more than a moment. If you do let it remain in one spot, you might as well be using a heavy sinker. Such an unnatural stoppage in the natural, jerky, downstream progress of a worm is likely to serve as a warning to stream-wise trout. Don't figure that making it easy for the trout to sally up to a worm at its leisure will help your chances. If the latter argument were made, then worm dunking in a pool, with the bait motionless on the bottom, would be more successful. For consistent results, the worm must be moving naturally.

If you find that you have erred in judging the speed of the current, you often can correct your mistake while the worm is in the water. If, for instance, you have chosen too heavy a sinker and realize that the sinker and worm are lagging in their downstream progress, it is a simple matter to tighten up your line slightly and gently drag the sinker

93

and worm downstream. In this case, drag prevents drag. If you have chosen too light a sinker, the worm and sinker may never reach the bottom at the suspected hide.

There is no doubt that worms dropping naturally into the stream from some earth clump sometimes will be swept downstream slightly above the bottom when the current is swift. So, a cast with too light a sinker is less likely to warn a trout than a cast with too heavy a sinker. When you determine your sinker is too light, there is a good chance that you can cast again with a heavier sinker and connect.

Throwing slack line when the worm is reaching the end of a good drift will permit the worm to drift several feet farther downstream before drag occurs.

Take the frequently encountered hide under a log, tree or bush projecting far out into the stream. You can't reach the best part of such hides with a true upstream cast. You have to let the worm slide downstream under the obstruction. With properly handled slack line you can do that effectively, permitting the worm to float naturally for as far as five or ten feet.

Many stream locations provide potential hides over a long distance. In such cases throwing slack line will permit you to cover more water in one drift with less danger of frightening a fish at the lower end of a drift, than when you lift out the worm with glaring unnaturalness.

Long hides would include, for instance, a log paralleling the current or a deeply undercut bank. Even a big bush hanging into the water has fish potential at almost any point.

When you throw slack line in covering a small pocket, you are permitting the worm to drift out of the trout's probable range of vision before you sound a potential warning by lifting the worm. A second try then is more likely to be successful.

Both in placing and lifting the worm, try to make as little disturbance as possible. Even though trout may not be able to see a worm and sinker that have been splashed into the water or sucked out of the water carelessly, they almost certainly can hear or feel the disturbance. Particularly in placing your worm, try to lay it down as gently as you would a dry fly. It can be done and it pays off. Raise your worm up from the bottom at the end of a drift just as gently.

On Eastern streams, at least, rainbow and brook trout do not respond as well as browns to the naturally-floated worm. Both brookies and rainbows are less wary than browns and much more inclined to lie in open water. Sometimes they actually seem to prefer a worm that is swinging sidewise in the current, or lying motionless on the bottom.

Both rainbows and brookies, however, still are trout. They are sensitive fish, if relatively stupid at times. You will take many more of them with skilled approaches, careful study of the stream and light tackle than you will by mere dunking, even though dunking often will produce brookies on certain streams and lakes. I have often fished for cutthroat trout and generally find them easy to take with flies. On the few occasions that a fly hasn't worked, spinning lures have.

On the subject of rainbow trout, New York State's renowned Catherine Creek offers a few lessons. This creek, so famous for its spring run of big rainbows, is hardly a trout stream in the true sense. The fish in that stream are primarily spawners. They are not interested in food. Trout fishing on this stream is not true trout fishing. But it does offer thousands of anglers, who jam the short stream each year, their first chance to escape from the stifling confinement of winter. And the trout do run large. Many are taken each spring that weigh eight to ten pounds and more.

To me, Catherine Creek is an outdoorsman's honky-tonk carnival. Somehow, while I'm fishing on that stream, for a few days at least, I can enjoy fishing pools even though I'm lined up shoulder to shoulder with other anglers. Real fishing or not, there is an eager gold-rush atmosphere that can't fail to excite you.

Only a relatively few anglers take the big fish. My success definitely has not been consistent. The success of other good wormers has been no more consistent than mine. But, several years ago, Ivor Evans and I did learn a few of Catherine Creek's secrets from Tom and Lyman Gibbs of Elmira, who probably take as many big rainbows from Catherine Creek regularly each year as most anglers on the stream take in a lifetime.

Ivor, the Gibbs brothers, and I were having coffee in a restaurant bordering the stream one cold, snowy day when the Gibbs boys offered to demonstrate how to catch a rainbow quickly. They said they were sure they could catch one from the pool directly behind the restaurant. We hadn't had a strike that morning despite our best brown-trout techniques. We were skeptical but willing to be shown.

Tom Gibbs waded a little way into the water and cast a long line quartering upstream so that his bait would go through a deep hole next to a mass of tree roots. He used much more lead than we had been using. The bait caught frequently on the bottom and remained there until he pulled it free.

There was much stream drag on his line which, for most of the drift, bellied deeply in the fast current. His line was tight at all times. He made no attempt to avoid drag. Later, he told me that a high proportion of the rainbows take his bait while it is sweeping around slowly at the end of each drift.

Tom didn't take a trout from that pool, but on his second drift he did snag into a whopper. He lost the fish though he landed one of about six pounds in the next pool downstream a few minutes later. The basic difference in his fishing method was a deliberate, but slight cross-stream drag. Apparently, that drag is exciting to these spawning fish, which you try more to irritate than to lure through their appetites. But I've seen that cross-stream drag work, too, on feeding rainbows in other streams during mid-summer.

Ivor and I wasted no more time after Tom landed his fish. Comparing notes later, we both found it difficult to break the habits it had taken us so many years to develop. Even though we tried, we subconsciously found ourselves trying to avoid line drag unless we made a determined effort. Both of us must have succeeded, partly at least, because we both began getting strikes soon after. After two days of being skunked, we both landed good trout. We've used that lesson to good advantage in subsequent years on Catherine Creek. It has helped sometimes on other rainbow streams.

chapter 15

Pause Before You Cast

ONE PRACTICE OF ALEC HENDERSON'S THAT STOOD OUT most clearly in our minds while we watched his movements from a distance was the long, motionless waiting periods he would make before a cast.

I recall how impatient I'd become, how I wondered why in heck Alec was wasting so much time before he'd finally raise his long rod into position for one of his delicate, precise casts.

I have no doubt that those waiting periods were a big factor in Alec's success. Neither do I have any doubt that it is a factor in the success of Dave Evans. I know that long waits before I have made casts have yielded me some fine fish. I know I should do it more often, continuously in fact, but, somehow, I guess I'm temperamentally unfitted for too much waiting.

When I know, or think I know, that there is a trout lying virtually under my rod tip, I find it extremely difficult to avoid trying for it as soon as I get into position. It is true that I take a great deal of time to work myself carefully into that position. Maybe that is why I have reasonably good success with worming in spite of my inability to wait a few minutes before casting. If I could quell my impatience, I'm sure I'd do better. Call it my angling weakness, but it's there and I doubt I'll ever be able to do much about it. In this case, I suggest you do as I preach, not as I do.

Alec's reasoning was obvious. Dave talked about it often during our winter bull sessions in the early days when we first took up worming seriously.

There is no doubt that an angler's movements along the banks of a stream or in the stream itself create some disturbance, no matter how careful he may be. There will be vibrations of the ground on which he walks, the slight crunching of pebbles under his feet, the ripples he creates on quiet water with his advancing boots. No matter how slowly he moves, he'll frighten chubs and suckers from the shallows into the pool or hide he intends to fish.

No one of these disturbances may amount to much. Each might be unimportant. With a good approach, there's a fair chance that none of these disturbances will frighten a trout. But there's also a good chance that, while that trout may not be frightened, it may become suspicious that something is not as it should be. After all, a trout is highly sensitive and, like most wild creatures, must be on constant guard against many potential enemies.

If you can assume that you create only suspicious, not frightening, conditions, then you can also assume safely, I think, that a trout's suspicions will fade a short time after the disturbances cease.

After all, minor disturbances obviously are a normal part of a trout's life. To a fish, there always are such things as gravel or mud sliding from an eroding bank, a rock shifting in fast current, a dead limb falling from a tree, a clump of grass dislodged by a muskrat upstream.

So, if you'll wait five, preferably ten minutes, before fishing each good hide, you permit the stream to return to normal and you improve your chances.

I've found one way to force myself to stand quietly for short periods before making my cast. That is to wait until I've worked myself into position before checking—and probably changing—my sinker weight. I also select and put a worm on the hook after I've reached my chosen position, providing I don't have a nicely-wiggling worm already impaled. Lighting a cigarette also helps slow me down.

Weakness or not, I'll force myself to stand or kneel quietly for at least a few minutes if I see I've caused ripples to swell through a hide, or have frightened a chub or sunning sucker into a hole. Those must be clear-cut warning signals to any trout.

The best bet, of course, is to assume that you have created a slight disturbance and permit the stream to quiet down completely before you cast. Try not to shift position to cast after you have taken the time to let the pool quiet down. Select your position in such a way that, after the quieting-down period, you can fish all or most of the best portions of the pool without moving. This is a tip that will help many fly anglers, too, but is more applicable to wormers because of the short line so preferable in effective worming.

One lovely day on moody Mansfield Creek, Dave Evans established to my complete satisfaction—and a certain amount of humiliation—the desirability of a waiting period. There was no question about it.

We had fished the stream from dawn. We both had nice fish and had released many others. It was around 11:00 A.M. and I was entering that careless stage where I was becoming as much interested in the natural beauties and sounds around me as I was in fishing. I saw Dave coming upstream as I waded into position slightly downstream from a small, fallen tree that had become imbedded on the bottom at a curve in the stream.

A shallow ripple ran into the small pool that the fallen tree had created. There was a nice curl of water under the tree trunk at its upstream end. Near the tail end, the water became glassy and I could plainly see branches of a tree a foot under the surface. Maybe I frightened chubs but I know I created a ripple as I entered that pool. I didn't wait. My two casts were good, the drifts were good, but there was no response.

Dave, meanwhile, had come abreast. Considerately, he was far back on the bank. I waded out of the pool and joined him for a smoke. We compared notes. Then, after about ten minutes, Dave mused: "You know, Jerry, I think you've run up against that careless period of yours. You sure cast in a helluva hurry when you fished that last pool. I think I'll give it a try."

I sat contentedly on the bank and watched. Dave seldom lets down. He's a perfectionist from the time he starts fishing until he ends the day. Every move he makes is smooth, deliberate, skilled.

Dave eased into the pool, stopping in almost exactly the same position I had selected. He became motionless, but we continued to converse. We've never found that talking disturbs trout. Dave must have waited ten minutes before he cast, again in almost the identical spot I'd selected for placing my worm.

I could see the telltale slackening of his line as the worm reached the bottom then, almost immediately, a decisive sideway movement of the line under the tree trunk. Dave struck and the battle was on. Dave waded out to the bank

and exerted a powerful downstream pressure, but the trout
continued to bore into its hide. He couldn't move the fish.
Suddenly it ripped out of the hide. I could hear the line
swish through the water as the fish raced downstream.

Dave followed along the bank. The fish made it to a
fast chute of water leading to another tree-covered pool.
It went downstream through the chute into the pool, then
sulked. That fish never jumped although it was hooked
only lightly. It thrashed a bit and bored for several more
minutes before Dave led it into his net in the shallows. It
was a nice sixteen-incher. Dave smiled at me, triumphantly
I'm sure, but he said nothing to twist the knife.

"You win," I grinned. "I'll try to do better."

chapter 16

Using Your Head

THERE IS NO SUBSTITUTE FOR USING YOUR HEAD. I KNOW quite a few wormers who go through all the mechanical motions of worming with apparent perfection but who have only moderate success. I've fished with many of these, watched them, talked to them at length. When they do poorly, when even normally good wormers do poorly, the answer usually lies in a lack of concentration, in a failure to use the old bean.

If your thoughts on a trout stream stray, if you are wondering, perhaps, whether you should have called in a doctor for your baby's cough or you are mentally debating whether your boss was fair the previous day in that bawling out he gave you, you can expect poor results with the trout.

Normally, trout fishing can divert you from your troubles as well or better than any other sport. There are many delightful problems and situations to solve on a stream that can become so absorbing that you will forget all else.

If you fish in this way, watching constantly for opportunities, studying the water, planning skilled approaches
to hides and observing (in order to establish a pattern)
the points in pools and riffles where you are getting the
most action, you may end up the day physically tired but
with your mind soothed. Even though he knows every
trick in the book, a consistently successful wormer must
also use his head. I, for one, will always do much better
on a day in which I have few worries or am able to shake
them off.

Such concentration, observation, and study cannot be
continued for any long period. I usually find myself starting to get a little careless, a little sloppy, after three or
four hours of hard fishing. Then, I'll find myself stumbling
past good hides, frightening trout out of spots I'd normally
be fishing properly, paying much more attention to the
thrilling drumming of a nearby grouse, the tangy odor of
the peppermint bed through which I may be walking, the
flavor of the wild strawberries I may spot as I start to
slip over a grassy bank. I love those things, too, and I
usually have all the fish I want anyway after three or
four hours of hard fishing.

Any fishing I do after those first hours usually is lacka-
daisical—spending time in an environment that charms me
more than any other. The fish then become incidental.
But in those hours of concentration, in that period when
the outwitting of a wily quarry is the major objective,
nothing else intrudes very much into my consciousness.
The Evans brothers tell me that trout fishing affects them
the same way.

In addition to watching the stream for second-best hides,
studying approaches and water currents, the desirability
of establishing stream patterns is highly important. For

instance, you may note on a certain day that the first fish you take walloped a very small worm; that you are getting no strikes in the next few hides on a larger worm.

Maybe the size of the worm makes no difference; maybe it does. Try a very small worm again. If you get a strike quickly on the small worm, it is quite likely you have solved one pattern for that stream on that particular day.

The strong tendency of all trout in one stretch of stream to act and feed as their brothers do at any moment of the day is something you can use to advantage at any time. Fly anglers utilize this knowledge constantly.

If one or two trout will take a No. 14 light Cahill dry fly fastened to a 4X tippet, the dry-fly man can figure reasonably that other trout will take it. If he gets more rises to his fly at the tails of pools than at the heads of pools, he can safely assume he'll continue to get most of his rises at the tails of pools. So he'll concentrate his attentions in such places until some new condition or observation suggests a change.

Similarly, the wormer must seek to determine the stream patterns of the hour. He has even more patterns to establish than the fly man, who is more concerned with surface or near-surface conditions.

You may find on a bright day that you are taking trout only from deeply shaded hides on one side of a stream. Trout on the sunny side of the stream are not moving. If you suspect that, use your time most advantageously by concentrating on the shady side of the stream. You may note that you are not getting many strikes when the shadows of small clouds pass over the water. If that's the case, wait a few moments after the shadow passes before making your cast.

You may find, particularly before the sun rises, and

in periods of discolored water, that trout are not in their accustomed hides but are cruising the riffles or lurking at the heads of pools where the riffles enter.

The possible variations of trout conduct are countless. That's what gives trout fishing its allure. If it were easy, if you could always count on trout to do the same thing, many of us probably would quit the game for a sport that offered a more interesting challenge.

In using your head on trout, you must try to consider every possibility that may be preventing you from taking these wily fish. You should even question practices suggested in this book for everyday angling, such as the desirability of keeping the worm on the bottom of the stream. I've taken many trout under unusual conditions, such as that dead-water pool on the Ausable, with an unweighted worm.

There is no substitute for observation, analysis and willingness to experiment. Detailed knowledge of the characteristics of individual streams is much more important to success than a general knowledge of many streams.

A good trouter, whether he is a fly man or a wormer, will almost always do better on water that he knows intimately than an equally skillful man who doesn't know the stream in such detail. By knowing a stream, I mean not only the location of the pools and hides and the stretches with the best fish but, more particularly, the moods of trout in such streams.

I've noted, for instance, that trout on the Esopus are particularly sensitive to the shadows of passing clouds. Trout in the gin-like waters of Mansfield and Clear Creeks in Western New York seem particularly sensitive to barometric changes. Trout on Michigan's Au Sable seem to move best in the evening after an extremely hot day.

They are very difficult to catch with any lure during daytime hours.

On the Firehole in Yellowstone Park, you can see dozens of fish rising during the summer months but, like many other anglers, you find yourself unable to produce a fly of any size that will take a single fish. However, all the good fly men will take many fish the next day. There are many such moody streams throughout the country. Head-work sometimes will solve the problems, sometimes nothing will help. But it's fun to try to figure out something that maybe the other fellow hasn't. There's something competitive in such figuring. If you find the answer, it's just as gratifying to the ego as breaking eighty on the golf course.

chapter 17

Stream Approach

THERE IS NO SINGLE FACTOR IN SUCCESSFUL WORMING FOR brown trout that is more important than the way in which you approach a pool or suspected hide and the position you select for fishing that drift.

Relatively little has been written about stream approach because most trouting articles concern fly men. To them, the approach is less important than to the wormer, who should strive to wade as closely to a trout as possible without frightening it. At the same time, stream approach is a consideration that should be given much more weight by fly anglers because a fly cast on a short line generally will produce better results and better fish than a fly cast on a long line. A skilled approach makes a short line possible for a fly man, too.

If there is any single practice that will tend to offset mistakes in other directions, it is good stream approach.

Nothing has occupied my attention more or provided greater interest in thirty years of intensive trout angling. I'm sure it is the study of stream approach that has enabled

me to keep approximately abreast in trouting success with
such skilled wormers as Dave and Ivor Evans, who do a
better job in other directions.

I doubt if anyone is more skilled than Ivor, for instance,
in his uncanny ability to float a worm naturally through
stream tangles that would mean a snagged hook or sinker
for me. His delicacy in lifting a worm almost immediately
from a grasping branch verges on the phenomenal. I've
watched this ability for years, admired it, tried to emulate,
but he's way ahead of me and his brother, Dave, in this
regard.

Dave surpasses all of us in the dainty way he can lay
a worm on quiet waters, in his patience in waiting long
minutes while he permits pools to settle down. Dave can
place a worm and sinker on the water as lightly as most
fly men can present a trout fly.

Non-fishing friends still rib me for some of the methods
I've used to study stream approach. I suppose I'll never
live down events on a summer day in which a large, mixed
party held an all-day picnic and swim on the shores of
Lake Erie.

Every trout angler has heard or read about a trout's
"window"—the surface area directly above a trout through
which it can see. Outside of that circular area, the surface
becomes opaque and the trout cannot see. Theoretically,
at least, if you keep yourself in that opaque area, in relation to the trout, you can move around with little danger
of the trout spotting you.

Much was being written about this "window" those
days. Outdoor magazines also were printing many articles
about the ability or inability of trout to detect colors in
flies. The day on Lake Erie gave me an opportunity to
check some of those theories.

After all, I had to make the best of that day on the

beach. It wasn't my idea. I'd rather have been on a trout stream. But a husband and father has to consider his family's wishes once in a while. Anyway, I stuck into the pocket of a light jacket a large box of assorted flies, both dry and wet.

It was a gay picnic but I ran into a hornet's nest of kidding when, during two different swims, I strolled up the beach to my jacket, as nonchalantly as possible, and withdrew the box of flies. Then, with the box held slightly behind me so I wouldn't be too obvious, I waded back out into the water, deliberately trying to stay away from the main group. The water was exceptionally calm. It was as glassy as most trout pools, differing from a trout pool only in the slight swell.

I beckoned to my long-suffering wife and she came over beside me. The water was about chest deep. I asked her to hold the box of flies after I selected a bright Parmachene Belle for my first test.

She was thoroughly amused and, instead of helping me conduct my experiments in secret, she sang out to the group to watch what "this nut is doing." I had to take it that day but the results of my experiments were both interesting and revealing.

At first, I was most interested in what a human eye could determine about the color of flies when it is underwater. I took a deep breath and sank, grabbing a loose rock on the bottom to hold me down. I kept one hand above the surface and dropped the Parmachene Belle into the "window." I could see it plainly. The slightly-bent hackles that penetrated the surface looked somewhat darker than the rest of the fly but I could not detect color. The scarlet of the fly appeared to my eyes, and I am definitely not color blind, as a medium shade of gray. The whites on the fly looked white. I tried other patterns. All colors looked to me like white, black, or shades of gray. That led me to the conviction that, color blind or not, a trout cannot detect colors in a dry fly.

Then I tried wet flies, holding them under water in front of me. I had no difficulty determining the approximate colors of any of the wet flies. That led to the conclusion that, if trout aren't color blind, they certainly can see colors under water as well as I could.

Then I started to study the "window." The deeper I sank, the wider the circumference of the "window," but the angles at which I could see above the surface didn't seem to change. Almost as if they were in a shimmering cloud, a little unreal, I could see the movements of my hand held in the open air above the "window." Vaguely, I could see my wife looking down at me. She was really amused. She's no trout angler. But she was tolerant.

I shifted my interest to the opaque area. I started moving my arm and hand through it. Again, my arm looked slightly darker where it penetrated the surface but I couldn't see beyond the surface. Outside the "window," the surface appeared a grayish white. My eye couldn't penetrate it even slightly.

As I moved my head closer to the surface, the circular "window" narrowed. I couldn't see as far to the side. If I splashed water in the "window" with my hand, the "window" closed until the water quieted.

Those tests impressed me. I've recalled them frequently during the thousands of hours I've spent since on trout streams. A strong realization of the presence of that "window" became the basic thought in my study of stream approach. There's nothing new in that for any good trout angler, but you do have to start somewhere. The eventual goal for a wormer or short-line fly fisherman is to squeeze to the limit—to get up to the edge of that window or, better yet, to utilize every type of screen possible to shield you from the eyes of a trout. At the same time you must do everything possible to prevent a trout from hearing you or feeling you.

The ability of a trout to feel practically soundless vibrations is well known. I had a good illustration of that one lazy, spring day on Clear Creek while fishing with Fred Turner. Fred is an older man but exceptionally graceful considering his six feet four inches, and his hulking frame. He never started serious trout fishing until he was sixty but his enthusiasm in trying to learn since that time has been a delight to me. He's a wonderful companion but, in spite of my best efforts, he keeps forgetting things.

If he concentrates on stream approach, he's liable to be careless with line drag. If he spots the second-best hides, which I've emphasized for so many years, he may be careless in his approach. Once in a while he'll do everything right and come back with some dandy catches.

On that day, I didn't care whether I caught trout or not. The balmy breeze was gentle, thorn apples were in bloom, countless mating songbirds were singing cheerily and crickets rasped. I walked along the stream enjoying the sights and sounds and smells of spring, idly picking up peppermint leaves to crunch in my fingers and hold to my nose, watching the antics of a noisy, distressed sandpiper obviously trying to lead me away from a nearby nest, drinking in deep the sweet odor of a field of clover.

I jumped a bunch of frogs in a small pool near the bank of the stream and sat down to see how long it would take before they'd reappear. Then I came to a pool in which I'd lost a good fish the week before. I crept up to the edge of the high bank on one side. A high bank is a position you want to avoid assiduously if you intend to fish a pool immediately, but this day I didn't care. As I neared the edge, I got on my stomach. I removed my cap and very slowly eased my eyes over the edge. Below me was the same tree stump from under which I'd hooked the good trout. A spring freshet had uncovered the roots and formed a nice pocket of water under them. Though the water was like gin, I saw no trout for a few moments, only a few chubs and a sucker in the tail of the pool.

Then I made out a trout, finning gently under the tree roots. It probably was the same fish I'd lost. As I continued to watch, several other trout became visible. All of them were good "keepers."

I had dropped Fred off a mile downstream from the point at which I parked the car. I had planned to walk downstream several hundred yards, then start fishing back to the car. But I never did get to start fishing until that afternoon. As I watched the trout, from a prone position, I also saw Fred ambling toward me, fishing stream pockets as he came. He came to a long, shallow riffle downstream from the pool at which I was lying.

"What in hell are you doing there?" exclaimed Fred as he walked heavily toward me alongside the shallow riffle. I waited for him to come closer before answering and my eyes strayed back to the fish.

Fred was at least seventy-five feet from me when the trout started to feel his presence. He was making no attempt to walk gently. I couldn't hear them at that distance but knew that, if I were closer, I would have been able to detect the muffled thumping of his boots on the soft, grassy turf. I doubt that even a sensitive trout could have heard Fred's steps at that distance, but the fish did start to shift around nervously. By the time Fred came up to me, they had disappeared, probably under the stump.

I had waved Fred away from the edge of the stream and motioned him to be quiet. But even though we waited a full half-hour before Fred tried the pool from the other side of the stream, he didn't get a touch.

Walking gently at all times, whether near a hide or not, is a vital requisite along most streams. Try to cultivate that soft, gliding walk of a woodland Indian even though it may tire some leg muscles you never knew you had.

If you can't develop that walk, you can set down your heels softly if you make a determined effort and walk slowly. You are trying to outwit trout, not win a marathon. Take it easy, particularly on gently flowing trout streams. You can get away with murder in walking along the gushing, tumbling type of stream.

The closer you are to a hide, the quieter the water, the more care you must use. If you are wading in the water, it pays off handsomely if you'll make each step with great deliberation, carefully choosing the point at which you'll make the next step so you do not stub your toe on a rock, grind gravel too noisily or create too much of a wake.

With our "window" constantly in mind, we obviously approach a hide from the lowest point possible. That, of course, always means the low-bank side of a stream. Only a rank amateur will even attempt to fish a pool from the high bank of a stream unless its depth or speed of current prevents you from crossing to the low side.

When you are on the high bank, you almost certainly will be in a trout's "window" as soon as it emerges from its hide. On both large and small streams, you'll run into situations now and then when you simply cannot fish from the low side of the stream. Then you'll have to count on an overhanging hide to shield you from view and to expose as little of your body as possible. Even though possible, as it sometimes is, to hook as many trout from a high bank by exposing to the fish's view little more than the rod, you have much more difficulty in playing and landing a good fish. From such a position, it is almost impossible to prevent a good fish from boring right back to the hide from which it came, maybe under the bank from which you are fishing. You have no leverage to stop it. You can apply pressure only upstream or downstream. You can't stop cross-stream movements of a powerful fish.

Sometimes you'll be fishing a stream with high banks on both sides. The only answer there is to remain in the water, depth permitting, and hope for the best. You simply can't come over the tops of high banks casually, drop into a stream and expect to catch many fish. The only partial answer to that problem is crawling, even wiggling on your stomach.

I've worn out many a pair of boots at the knees before the soles were shot. It is a rare day in which I don't feel a cool trickle of unwanted water on my thighs as I edge on my knees through shallow runs of water toward an alluring hide. That "window" stands out constantly before me and I'll do almost anything to keep my silhouette low.

On a trout stream, I think I'm on my knees, my rump, and sometimes my stomach almost as much as I am on my feet. When I am on my feet and approaching a hide, I usually keep my head and shoulders hunched well over, sneaky-Indian fashion. Those practices usually mean sore knees, an aching back, and scraped hands but they also help greatly to increase the weight of your creel. Three or four hours of that kind of hard, intensive, try-to-do-everything-right fishing generally will yield far more and better fish than dawn-to-dusk careless angling.

Walking quietly, staying on the low side of a stream, and keeping your body silhouette low when making your approach are fundamental. The real technique in stream approach is in learning just how closely you can safely come to a hide and how low you must keep your body.

Much of that depends on your stealth and, probably even more important, on the screen that you use to shield you from the trout's vision.

For practical angling, there is no better screen than ripples on the water. If the ripples are sharp, they'll usually close the trout's "window" quite decisively. If you abuse this knowledge on gentle ripples, you may get into trouble. My experiments on Lake Erie indicated that you could get a suggestion of movement above the surface when the water was disturbed only slightly. Here you must use some judgment.

Under cover of sharp wind-created ripples, I've often succeeded in stalking up within two or three feet of small trout, usually rainbows or brookies, lying out in open water. I had no idea these trout were there. Every time it has happened, I was getting into position to fish a hide. I saw these fish because the wind that created the ripple had died down for a moment and permitted me to look under the surface of the water at the same time it was opening up the trout "window."

Those close approaches to fish lying in open water provided a good lesson. I found that if I stood perfectly still when the "window" opened, the trout often would be undisturbed. They'd just hold their positions in the current, gently moving their fins. That hasn't always held true. Some of these trout have scooted off as if the devil were after them with a pitchfork. But enough have stayed to indicate the value of freezing in your position if the wind-created ripple you are using for an approach suddenly becomes a glassy surface.

I've often wondered why those trout which permit you to approach so closely are not disturbed by the movements of your waders and boots under the surface, gentle as those movements may be. I can only theorize. Even though virtually all my casts are cross-stream, or up and across, I always work upstream on any river or creek.

A trout headed upstream, as it must be to hold its position in the current, is less likely to detect movements to its rear—downstream. Also, working upstream eliminates the danger of your boots disturbing silt or sand and floating it in a cloud to a trout downstream which, without doubt, would regard the disturbance as suspicious, if not frightening.

In any event, I suspect that trout are more concerned with enemies that may strike from above, like kingfishers or blue herons, than enemies in the stream itself, like larger fish. If you approach them very gently from behind, the underwater movements need cause you no serious concern.

While puzzling over this relative lack of fear for underwater movements, I think of the several times I've seen farm boys reach their arms gently over a stream bank into an undercut hide and, after working their hands slowly and mysteriously for a few moments, come up with a squirming trout. In each case, they knew almost the exact location of the trout, having seen it dart into this particular hide previously.

They told me that they avoided touching a trout's tail. They tried to get their fingers under the trout's belly. That done, they stroked the trout's belly for a moment—something a trout apparently likes—and then worked their fingers toward the gills, where they could get a good grip.

One of the trout illegally grabbed in this way weighed three pounds. These are unbelievable and even shocking demonstrations, but they illustrate another of a trout's weaknesses. Why fingers touching a trout's belly wouldn't send it into panicky flight I'll never know. We'll leave that to an ichthyologist.

When you have decisive ripples, there is no need to go to extremes to keep your silhouette low. You can even stand upright without much danger, and, if you move slowly and very quietly, without gravel crunching, you can safely assume that you may approach within eight or ten feet of a suspected hide without disturbing the fish.

You may have a good cover of ripples on the side of the stream in which you are standing but the hide that is your object often will be in glassier water, like that pocket under the bushes near the far bank or the dark run under the log near the tail end of a pool. On such a setup, play it safe, and stay low.

No two hides or pools have identical water conditions. Each creates its own problem and offers a challenging opportunity for you to practice your stalking ability. Each time, it is a sort of game to be figured out, either consciously or subconsciously. If you win, you can't help beaming a little, inwardly at least.

One of the most interesting stalks I can remember was definitely a conscious one. In fact, the problem of that pool on startling-clear Mansfield Creek that summer was crystallized forcibly in my mind by the fact that the pool almost had Fred Turner and me stymied.

Mansfield trout, probably because of the clear water, are exceptionally sensitive. If you are careless, you sometimes can see them dart away when you are on a bank fifty feet away. For some reason, the "window" on this stream seems wider than it is on other streams. The sensitivity of these Mansfield trout and the clear water undoubtedly are the reasons why the stream contains some of the largest fish in Western New York. Catching them is the problem.

Fred spooked about a dozen nice trout in that particular pool the first time we fished the stream that summer. He had approached carefully, but not carefully enough. He told me about it as we were driving home that night.

The pool was a new one, apparently created in a spring freshet. Leading into the pool was a long, shallow, hideless riffle. This riffle slid quite gently into the pool and ran against an undercut clay-loam bank, abruptly turning to the right at a ninety-degree angle and sweeping gently along this bank in a glassy slick. The current ran for only a few feet along the bank, then eddied into a quiet pool that extended from the edge of the riffle, where it entered the pool, to a point about fifty feet downstream. All of that water was glassy and the quiet portion of the pool contained many chubs and suckers that would swarm up into the riffles, disturbing trout there, if you came within their vision.

Fred was eager to have me try that pool the next time we fished the Mansfield about a week later. He came along to watch. He didn't even bother to put his rod together.

When I studied the pool from a position well back on the lower bank, I knew we had a real problem. An approach from the high bank was obviously impossible. You could not approach from downstream. If you tried that, even sneaking along low near the shore, the chubs would spook the trout even if the trout didn't see you.

The best bet seemed to be an on-the-belly sneak to the high point of the lower bank, then a long cast, undesirable though that may be. I made my stalk in this way but, in an almost prone position, found it difficult to cast accurately and to keep drag out of the line after it was in the water. I succeeded in taking only one small trout but withdrew carefully from that position so I could make another try later in the day.

On the next try, I realized I had to do something completely unorthodox. The answer to that pool was a downstream approach through the riffles to a point near the head of the pool. From this position, I could reach out effectively to the apparent hot spot in the pool—the point where the riffle was curling into the undercut bank.

I saw a little cloud of silt at my boots discolor the pool slightly as I worked downstream, hunched well over at first, then slipping to one knee at the last.

The cloud of silt, of course, presumably had sent up the red flag to the trout and I forced myself to smoke a cigarette to the end. Even though the riffle was shallow, the current was curling water near my boot tops and I pulled them up as well as I could. Then I fastened an extra-lively blackhead worm to a worm gang, cast to a point several feet above the suspected hide, and immediately threw about five feet of slack line to prevent drag. I lowered the rod tip quickly to provide more slack.

A good trout snapped up the worm almost immediately and, instead of making its fight near the hide, obligingly tore downstream. It dashed around wildly there for a few minutes and made two relaxed-looking leaps. The trout never entered the ripples again. Remaining on one knee, I succeeded in leading it through quiet water near the lower bank and into my net at the edge of the riffles.

I reasoned there was a fair chance that other trout in the hide may not have been disturbed by the antics of this fish downstream. There was a chance that the chubs had not scattered into the riffles, where I knew the trout must be lying.

Incidentally, if you hook a chub from a hide or pool, you can figure your chances of taking a trout at that point have been reduced greatly. An unnaturally wiggling chub on a hook surely acts as a warning signal to nearby trout. Furthermore, if your cast was good and the trout wanted your worm, it would surely beat the chub to it.

Fred waited back on the bank as I hooked up another worm, and lightened my sinker slightly. I took a chance and cast without any further delay. Again, a nice trout took the worm almost immediately, but this one chose to fight it out in the ripple part of the pool. That ended fishing in that pool for the day.

Two days later, Fred approached the same pool in the same way and took two more fish after talking to some native anglers who hadn't even bothered to fish what they called "the spooky hole," even though they knew it contained better-than-average trout. They said they had fished it often, never succeeded in taking a trout from it. Obviously, they hadn't approached the pool properly.

Another such problem pool on the Ausable comes to mind, one of hundreds every trout angler will encounter in years of fishing.

The Ausable pool is also glassy for most of its length of about seventy-five feet. It lies along a brushy bank. An approach from the shore is impractical. Virtually all anglers who fish it wade in the shallow part of the pool near the brush. That is obvious, year after year, from the boot tracks in the sand.

The main stream is about one hundred and fifty feet wide at that point, most of it rushing along tempestuously past large boulders. A gravel bar just below the mouth of a cold brook entering the river, however, breaks the force of the river's current thus permitting formation of the glassy pool.

Joe Rigler had fished the pool a number of times before he took me to that stretch. He, too, had waded near the brush while fishing the pool. He'd taken some of the many nice trout that concentrated there in the cool water, but complained of the many trout he spooked, no matter how much care he used. He had tried to work around the outside edge of the pool, where the fast water riffles would shield him from the trout's view, but his rubber-bottomed boots were not adequate for the job. Joe's stubborn. No experienced angler will trust rubber-bottomed boots on the treacherously slippery rocks of the Ausable, but Joe always insisted that felt soles or chains were for "sissies." Joe has never hurt himself badly on the Ausable but, as in this pool, I knew he often was forced to approach good spots improperly because of inadequate footgear. On the Ausable I make a real "sissy" of myself and always carry a bamboo staff. I don't know how I could get along without it on that stream.

I doubt many anglers work that pool from the fast-water side. Even with felt-bottomed waders and a staff, the powerful current almost swept me downstream several times. Working upstream against it made me puff. But that clearly is the way to fish that particular spot.

On that first day and in the years since, I've never failed to take at least one sizable trout from it. On several occasions I could easily have taken a limit, I'm sure. As soon as I hooked trout there, I tried to lead them out into the fast water so they wouldn't disturb the pool. Then, they'd usually go downstream with the current. I'd merely wade downstream with them and land them below the tail of the pool. Then I'd wade back upstream into position.

This led to an amusing incident one nice July afternoon. Downstream I'd met another angler who hadn't taken a fish. He inquired about my luck and, when I told him I had "a few," asked if he could look in the creel. I had several fish weighing one to two pounds and he inquired about my methods and lure, then eagerly suggested that maybe I wouldn't mind if he came along and watched.

Somehow, I can't seem to fish as well when another angler is watching. The awareness of his presence seems to create a tension, a difficulty in concentration, but the trouble I got into on that day couldn't be blamed on the watching angler. It was just plain, awkward carelessness.

I led my acquaintance to that favorite glassy pool. He stood quietly on the bank while I waded into position. The first part of the lesson worked well. I hooked a good brownie on the second cast and, as usual, drew it out toward fast water. This trout, however, crossed me up. As soon as it reached fast water, it raced swiftly upstream about twenty feet. Then, just as quickly, it turned downstream, leaving me with a slack line. The trout dashed between my legs, spread wide because of the speed of the current, and then turned upstream again. The line tangled around one wader leg. I raised the leg to try to free the line. That did it. The current carried me off my feet and I fell backward into the water. I felt the cool water pouring into the waders and fought to regain my footing. When I did, I realized I still had the fish. I landed it. It was about thirteen inches.

With water dripping into my eyes from my wet hair, I turned to the bank to show my acquaintance. He was laughing uproariously, although I couldn't hear him above the roar of the water. I knew I had given him a helluva demonstration of how to do it and he obviously felt the same way. He started to walk away downstream, obviously with no further interest in such lessons. I never saw him again. I released the fish. It sure had given me a beating.

On some larger streams, like the Esopus, lower Beaverkill and the Ausable, a second-best approach sometimes will be as effective as fishing second-best hides. Those second-best approaches often will provide opportunities to fish effectively over fish that usually see only badly-dragging flies or worms.

Be constantly on the lookout for such second-best op-

portunities. You must find them if you want to do better
than average. Many other anglers are making the obvious
approaches, fishing the obvious hides. What you want in
heavily-fished streams is the less-obvious setup. Be a pisca-
torial rebel who refuses to follow the flock. It pays off.

There is a certain stretch on the Ausable that illustrates
well the desirability of a second-best approach. The water
on both sides of this stretch is shallow. In the approximate
center of the stream, however, are a number of large
boulders, the blackness under them indicating hides with
good potential. There is a waist-deep channel in the middle
of the stream with enough force to discourage most anglers
from crossing at that point.

With only one exception, every angler I have ever seen
fish that stretch has worked from the side of the river
bordered by a dirt road. The deep channel is quite narrow
and it is reasonably easy for a good caster to reach the
near side of almost all of the boulders. That's the way
most all of the anglers do it. It's the easy way, the logical
way.

It is perfectly natural and human to avoid making more
work out of fishing than necessary. So, being a rebel, I've
never fished that stretch from the easy side. I always grab
the old bamboo wading staff and cross to the other side.
I fish the hides under each of the boulders from the other
side and I'm seldom disappointed. An observant angler
would note that the odds would favor that other side. The
far sides of those boulders cast some shade during part of
each sunny day while the near sides are in almost constant
sunlight. A brownie, normally a night feeder, is going to
be much more inclined to feed in shade than in glaring
sunlight.

In thinking like a rebel in your stream approaches and

selection of hides, you'll frequently be called upon to make exceptions to rules.

We've emphasized the desirability of avoiding high banks as a point from which to fish; yet you'll run into circumstances where it is the only way of doing it effectively. Take those small meadow streams, where the water runs one or two feet below the surface of the ground and both banks are of approximately equal height.

On such a stream, you must use your own judgment continuously, and violate many of the suggestions made in this book for larger streams. Generally, you have to stay on top of the banks of such streams. For this reason, it is especially necessary to keep your body low. It often is desirable to spot your hide from a point many feet downstream, mark it carefully and then fish it from well back on the bank, with only the tip of your rod extending over the bank.

One important tip for meadow streams: even though you may hardly be able to hear your footsteps on the soft turf, make it a strict rule to walk softly. Turf seems to be one of the best conductors of foot vibrations.

Unorthodox approaches also are called for on brushy streams. On such streams, I've taken many a trout with a fly or worm dropped straight down from the tip of a rod that had been pushed carefully through a small opening in the brush. In such situations, you should also try to provide enough slack line to permit at least a short natural float.

chapter *18*

Spinning for Big Trout

ONLY NOW AND THEN WILL YOU HEAR OR READ ABOUT upstream spinning for trout. It is a relatively rare method, but one that will consistently outfish any other spinning technique on most trout streams.

This is said with the full knowledge that the common method of casting approximately cross-stream and permitting the lure to swing in an arc downstream is responsible for a high proportion of the big trout taken each year on many of the country's trout streams.

That method has been deadly, for instance, on the famed Au Sable of Michigan which, as recently as ten years ago, could hardly be surpassed anywhere in the country for large and scrappy brown and rainbow trout. Today, anglers with spinning tackle have made relatively rare the big fish that once were so common on the Au Sable. The Au Sable now must be regarded as a hard-fished stream, one in which it is as difficult to catch big trout as it is in the even harder fished streams of New York State, Pennsylvania, and the New England States. So be it.

Those trout provided much pleasure to the spin fisherman, even though the fly men may not have liked it. The spin fishermen undoubtedly took fish that the fly men wouldn't have taken anyway. Each man to his last, and may each get the utmost in pleasure from what he is doing without selfishly pious scorn for the pleasures of another man.

Tougher fishing conditions and increasing stream competition call for improved methods. Upstream spinning is much more deadly than cross-stream spinning, just as light-tackle worming is more deadly than worm-dunking. It is much simpler to learn than the worming technique.

You will hear much more about upstream spinning in years to come. It is to be recommended highly to the beginner at trout angling because there is no spinning method that will produce more trout on most streams, even if the angler has little stream knowledge. With only limited stream knowledge, an upstream spin fisherman, under certain conditions, can take trout in places where they cannot be taken with a fly, minnow, or worm. And, in certain periods of the year, the upstream spinner can outfish the best of wormers, even on streams that are ideal for worm-fishing.

As mentioned previously, these periods include a short period late in spring, when warming water causes minnows to become extremely active, and again late in the summer, when cooling waters bring the big trout out of their hang-outs for a pre-winter feeding splurge.

It is a notable fact that many of the largest trout on any stream are in still stretches. It may be that their selection of such stretches is the reason they become large fish. Nevertheless, those still waters are among the best places on a stream for big fish, even though all you may see in them is chubs, suckers, and minnows.

Fishing such still waters effectively with a fly or a worm often is extremely difficult, if not impossible. It requires the very finest tackle, the most skillful casting, and, more important, an approach that will not scatter the minnows and spook the trout. When there is no wind to blow up riffles on such a pool, you either must make very long casts or, in most cases, you might as well skip it.

Even if you can approach effectively, the chubs usually will drown the dry flies or gulp the wet flies and worms. Pools like that can be damnably frustrating for the fly or worm man. They can be just what the doctor ordered for the upstream spin angler.

I had my first personal contact with upstream spinning some years ago on my first fishing trip with Bucky Sieminski and Frank Cramer. Like our worming clique, these two, and several other Buffalo area anglers, had worked out the details of upstream spinning to the point where catches of large trout among them were becoming relatively common.

They did have days in the summer when they drew complete blanks, however, and it was a nice catch of trout I took on worms on one such day that drew us together. They wanted to learn the worming technique.

Frank never did take up worming seriously. I suspect he found it too difficult. But Buck was one of the best pupils I ever had. He had been trouting only a few years but his boyish enthusiasm and his amazing ability to learn quickly enabled him to become a fine wormer in a few months.

Meanwhile, I was learning something, too. On our first trips together, Buck still was skeptical about worming in comparison with spinning, so he didn't even bother to acquire worming tackle. He brought only spinning tackle. Wisely, he'd follow me along the stream for several hours, sometimes using my rod, but usually doing little more than watching and asking questions.

Then he'd get his spinning rod and go off by himself. The fish he'd bring back sometimes topped anything I'd take with worms. That didn't happen often, except during the late summer. Then he and Frank usually would outfish me. So—well, I started to follow Buck along the stream. A short time after, I started to acquire spinning tackle.

There's no doubt about it. Under certain conditions, upstream spinning is deadly. Even on small streams, the size of the fish you can take with spinning lures fished upstream sometimes is unbelievable. Three and four pounders are relatively common. One of the clique, Bob Bromnick, took a ten and one-half pounder from Ontario's Credit River in the summer of 1957.

Fundamentally, upstream spinning differs from other types of spinning only in the direction in which the lure is cast in relation to the stream. You cast upstream, as directly upstream as possible, then reel like mad in a fast current to give your lure some action and prevent it from catching on the bottom. That's why a spinning reel with a fast rate of retrieve is essential.

To those not familiar with upstream spinning, there is a welcome surprise in store. It was a welcome surprise to me, too.

Of course, there is much more to upstream spinning than the direction in which the lure is cast. Nevertheless, we'll repeat that it can produce fine trouting results for a tyro more quickly than any other method of angling. By comparison with the techniques you have to learn to become a good wormer, or even a good fly man, it's a cinch.

I'm from Missouri but eager to try anything new in trout angling. It's for sure that when we learn all there is

to know about a sport, we tend to lose interest. In trouting no human will ever know all the quirks and vagaries
of his quarry. If he did, there would be no element of
chance, no feeling of accomplishment in having outwitted
a wily opponent. Trout angling would then become no
more satisfying than netting fish from a hatchery pool.
We'd quit angling for a more challenging sport.

Buck's and Frank's method interested me greatly but,
like most experimenters, I wasn't satisfied that their technique was the best until I had also tried more conventional
spinning methods over a period of several seasons. I'm
convinced now.

Buck gave me one of the most conclusive demonstrations of the effectiveness of the upstream method one
late-August day on lower Ischua Creek.

For several nights there had been a suggestion of frost
in the air. Then, after a light rain one night, it turned
warm again. The breeze on this day had that special, soft,
soothing quality that makes you glad to be alive.

We started fishing near dawn. I let Buck out of the car
at a certain bridge crossing the Ischua and drove upstream
several miles to another bridge. He would fish upstream
to the car; I'd go downstream to the bridge where he had
started. Then he'd drive the car downstream and pick
me up at noon.

Normally, we don't work it that way because we
usually find it preferable not to fish over water that has
just been fished by a partner. But I wanted to compare
the effectiveness of upstream and downstream spinning
so, on this day, we worked it out that way.

Buck is more accurate with a spinning rod than I am.
I'm sure he could throw lures into a bushel basket almost
every time at a distance of fifty to seventy-five feet, even
in high winds. He casts accurately from any position that

seems advisable, including right-handed side casts across his body. He's good. That may have made some difference on that day but, while I'm not in Buck's class as a caster, I was placing my lures quite accurately.

Anyway, when I met him coming upstream, I could see his creel sagging heavily. He had three beautiful brownies and had released six other good "keepers." I had several fish but they weren't even comparable with Buck's.

We had agreed to try not to disturb promising hides and I continued downstream over water Buck had fished. He told me the exact location of two pools in which two good trout had followed his lure out from a hide but had not taken. I tried hard and fished those particular pools with all the skill I possessed. I took only two seven-inch trout in the stretch over which Buck had already fished.

When Buck drove up, he was beaming with his boyish grin. He had taken two more good fish in the stretch which I had covered first. One of the fish was a fat eighteen-incher.

Other experiments with downstream spinning on other days and other streams were not so conclusive as that, but there was no doubt that both Buck and Frank would outfish me if I persisted in downstream spinning. Frank was no better caster than I. I finally bowed completely.

There are many good reasons why upstream spinning will do a better job than fishing lures across a stream and permitting them to swing down.

In the first place, a lure coming downstream to a trout is moving in the direction that most of a trout's food moves. That comment, of course, does not hold true if you are referring to minnows, which will move in all directions. If you are using lures simulating a minnow, the relative advantages of upstream spinning are less pronounced. But for some reason the advantage still exists.

Most trout anglers, including myself, have regarded larger trout as relatively slow-moving fish in comparison with smaller trout. We usually expect them to dimple a water gently in taking a dry fly, to suck in a worm deliberately, not with the fire and dash of a smaller fish. Upstream spinning will provide a revelation to you in the speed of big trout. It is amazing how swiftly they can and will flash up to take a lure moving rapidly downstream past their lair. A fast-moving lure doesn't give the trout time to think about whether it wants it or not.

Buck has always insisted that Frank reels in a lure too slowly. Buck insists that a rapidly moving lure doesn't give a trout time to study it and, possibly, reject it. It sees the lure coming, it looks like a good food possibility and it reacts. I think Buck is right. Fast reeling now produces much better results for me than reeling just fast enough to keep the lure wobbling or spinning.

There are days, however, when slower reeling pays off handsomely for Frank. Furthermore, he'll often end up a trout season with the largest trout taken by any of the spinning gang on Western New York streams. On the average, however, Buck's fast reeling will produce at least double the poundage of Frank's fish. And there are few seasons in which Buck doesn't land a number of three and four-pound trout. In the first week of the 1958 season, he took one that weighed four pounds, fifteen ounces.

None of us have figured out why Frank's slower reeling pays off at times. More particularly, we can't guess when slow reeling is advisable. Maybe you can puzzle out that one.

Another good reason for upstream spinning is that you can cover pools and hides much better than you can with downstream spinning. Not only can you go in close to a hide, but, if the hide is a long one, such as an extended undercut bank, you often can accurately fish the entire hide with one cast. The theory of placing a lure very close to a trout's hiding place, instead of just anywhere in a pool, holds good in spinning almost as much as in worming.

It is good practice in any type of trout angling not to try to force a trout to move out too far from its suspected hide. With upstream spinning, you will find more exceptions to this rule than in most other types of angling.

There are days in which you will see trout flash out for lures several feet from their hides. They'll often follow it downstream, without taking, almost to the tip of your rod. There's something particularly fascinating to a trout in a lure moving rapidly downstream. Generally, however, you will do much better if your lure is close to the hides.

The cross-stream spinner's lure obviously must swing in an arc, usually away from the hide as he maintains lure action by reeling in. On the other hand, an upstream spinner's lure is in "hot" water all the time.

Only rarely will a good brown trout strike a lure that is being reeled upstream against the current. As soon as a lure fished downstream completes its arc, it must be drawn upstream. For my money, all of that reeling-in time not only is wasted, but it is an almost sure way of spooking brown trout in that pool, even though you are using a minnow-type lure. Rainbow and brook trout often will provide outstanding exceptions to that rule, but it happens seldom with browns.

A lure fished upstream is potentially deadly from the time it enters the water until it reaches the rod tip. In addition, it is ready for another cast immediately and there has been no unnatural movement of the lure to spook a brown. You may cast again, although, as with worms, your first one or two properly made casts will produce the majority of fish you will take.

If you know a trout is lying in a certain hide and it does not take in two accurate casts, it is extremely unlikely that it will take in subsequent casts. In fact, I feel sure that subsequent casts will put down the fish even more firmly and make such a trout more difficult to catch if you decide to return and try for it later in the day.

Your time will be spent much more productively if you'll move on to the next hide, or another pocket in the same hide, after several casts in one place. Brown trout are not usually susceptible to nagging with a worm or lure although they do succumb at times to an artificial "hatch" created with a dry fly. Rainbow and brook trout can be nagged more successfully.

I've hooked many a rainbow trout with a spinning lure held unnaturally in the current a few inches upstream from a promising hide, but that method seldom will work on browns of any size.

chapter 19

Spinning Tackle
and Technique

THE MOST IMPORTANT PIECE OF UPSTREAM-SPINNING GEAR
is a dependable, open-spool reel with a fast retrieve. Luxor,
Mitchell, and Orvis reels with full bails are among the
favorites of our crowd.

I've experimented on many days with manual types of
spinning reels, which I prefer for all other spin fishing,
but this type of reel just will not do a consistently good
job for me on upstream spinning.

A cardinal requirement in upstream spinning is that
your lure must be moving toward you as soon as it hits
the water. Note that fact well. There cannot be a delay
of even a small fraction of a second. You should either
be reeling in or raising your rod tip on a tight line even
before the lure strikes the surface.

There is a logical explanation for this. If you can assume
that there is a trout that can see your lure when it splashes
into the water, you can also assume that the success of

135

that cast, insofar as that trout is concerned, will be decided
almost immediately. No one who has observed the mar-
velously fast reactions of a trout able to single out a tiny,
floating insect from a mass of other small bits of flotsam
floating down a stream, can question its reaction time.

The trout may be finning, apparently relaxed, in quiet
water behind a rock, while it watches dozens of small
pieces of twigs, buds, and grass seed float by in a rapid
current. Then, in a blur of movement almost too fast to
follow, it will dart out several feet into that current and
unerringly gobble up an insect too small for your eye to
see.

Every observant trout angler has seen instances of a
trout's fast reactions.

So, the fact must be kept in mind in fishing a spinning
lure. Undoubtedly, it is even more important to keep it
in mind with such a lure than it is with a fly, minnow,
worm, or plug because an unmoving spinning lure is about
as obviously phony as the falsies on the pretty girl while
she's bathing in a low-necked swimming suit.

Furthermore, starting the retrieve immediately permits
some other niceties in technique and prevents snagging on
the bottom. A typical nicety would be your ability to cast
to a point considerably upstream from a hide into a shallow
riffle. Such a cast would be made to muffle or drown the
sound of a lure splashing in the water. The lure, when
first seen by a trout in that pool, would be coming naturally down through the riffle.

That stunt is one of my contributions to the upstream
spinning technique. It is particularly effective when fishing
a glassy pool in which trout sometimes spook easily. I
first made the suggestion to Buck while I was following
him along a stream during my early days as an apprentice
upstream spin fisherman.

We were fishing a stretch of the East Koy below

Hermitage that day. On that section are many glassy pools and gentle riffles. Buck wasn't doing too well. At that time he was a little careless and driving his lure like a bullet into the water. His purpose, of course, was accuracy. Even in those days, he could place a lure into snaggy pockets and under overhanging tree limbs with a precision that was admirable. But his lures did splash, sometimes sharply. At that time, he didn't think it made much difference. It doesn't much of the time. At other times, it does. That was one of the times.

We came to a pool in which I had lost a good fish about ten days earlier. As usual, Buck placed his lure near the head of the pool and reeled it rapidly past a series of overhanging alders. Nothing happened. We hadn't seen any sign of a good fish in over an hour on similar pools. Only piddlers seemed to be on the move. After Buck's one cast, I suggested a smoke. We must have sat there a half-hour, during which I argued that casts into the riffles might improve Buck's chances of taking good browns in quiet pools like those he had been fishing.

Buck agreed that it could do no harm to try. It only meant casting a few more feet. The pool had had a long rest when Buck tried it again, this time casting to a point about five feet above the head of the pool. A trout had his weighted spinner almost as soon as it entered the pool. Buck landed it and looked at me with a how-do-you-like-that expression. Apparently, that trout had been lying at the very head of the pool. When the lure was first placed there, it must have splashed right on top of its head.

Many trout in a stream will do the same thing on the same day. Those are the kind of patterns you try to determine. It worked out that morning, too. Buck took several more nice fish within the next hour from the very heads of pools by casting into the riffles.

Starting the retrieve of your lure immediately also per-

mits you to fish effectively in places you wouldn't dare
try if you delayed your retrieve. There are places on many
streams, particularly small ones, where you can vaguely
see such booby traps for lures as underwater clumps of
brush, watersoaked logs and the like. These booby traps
also are fine hiding places for trout. If you can swim a
lure right over places like that, you'll often get a smashing
strike. If you delay in your retrieve, the lure, more often
than not, will snag on these obstructions and that ends
your chances in that hide.

It is the necessity for an immediate retrieve that inclines
me so strongly to the full-bail type of spinning reel. Yes,
with practice, you can retrieve immediately with the
manual-pickup reel, but I've never seen anyone who was
able to do it consistently, especially when a high wind is
tending to blow away the monofilament from your pickup
finger. Your finger often will miss the line on the very pool
in which you most want an immediate retrieve. Anyway,
it seems that way. In spin casting for bass or pike and even
in downstream casting for trout, the immediate retrieve is
less important and I still like a manual reel for those types
of fishing.

Many of the lures we use in upstream spinning weigh
only one-eighth of an ounce, sometimes less. We seldom
use lures weighing more than one-fourth ounce. That
means a light-action rod. Most of us prefer rods of seven
or seven and one-half feet. One of my favorite spinning
rods has so light an action that I sometimes use it for a
fly rod on small streams.

Most of us favor four-pound-test monofilament line for
day-in-and-day-out fishing but in very clear waters of late
summer shift over to three-pound-test. If these lines seem
on the heavy side for such light lures, remember that all
of us are constantly making a point of getting far back into

hides. If we used a very light line, desirable as that might be, we'd lose even more lures than we do. We lose plenty of them as it is.

To give you an idea of the number of lures we lose, Frank, Buck and I ordered and used up a full gross of one type of lure alone in two successive seasons. Most of those lures are lost when we deliberately break them off a snag or overhanging tree branch rather than disturb a good pool. That policy has paid off many times. A second, more accurate cast into that pool has produced good fish for us often enough so that we don't let ourselves be concerned over lure losses. The skinflint in me usually sends me out in search of lost lures after I've fished a pool thoroughly but, somehow, I don't seem to recover many of them.

On lures, we've found nothing better for most streams than the weighted spinners. These include the Heddon Hep, Mepps, and C. P. Swing. For most streams running at normal levels, one-eighth-ounce lures seem best but, for heavier water, we also use three-sixteenth-ounce and one-quarter-ounce lures. For most light conditions and most streams, we prefer the gold-finish spinners. Nickel and copper finishes also work well at times. A nickel finish is the best bet in discolored water.

We've never been able to figure out for sure what kind of natural trout food these spinners simulate. Sometimes, it seems that they represent minnow life. On some streams chubs will not touch them. That would bear out the theory that they appear to be minnows. On other streams or on other days, they seem to simulate insect life of some type because chubs will take them with enthusiasm. Maybe they are just some sort of mysterious, delectable-looking tidbit.

In any event, they are murderous on almost every stream. In both the one-eighth and one-fourth ounce sizes, depending on the depth of water and speed of current,

I've experimented with them for short periods on such
Western streams as the lower Madison, Gallatin, Yellowstone, Big Hole and Lewis Rivers, and found them just as
deadly as they are on Eastern streams. But, as I've indicated before, I strongly prefer flies on Western streams
and have used spinning lures on them only in those rare
times when I can't take trout on flies.

There are days in which the trout pattern swings in the
direction of minnows, particularly in the first series of
warm days in June. Then, such old favorites as the Devon
minnow, Thommen Dolly, Killer, Goldfish, Phoebe, and
Thomas lures will do an excellent job. Even then, trout
that we may raise and miss on the minnow lure often will
rise again and connect if we switch to weighted spinners.

Phil Savage and I had a convincing demonstration of the
effectiveness of upstream spinning on the beautiful, but
little-known De Grasse River in Northern New York one
day early in June a few years after I had learned the technique. The De Grasse is spectacular over much of its
length. There are lovely waterfalls, with deep pools below,
rock chasms, big boulders, and wild rapids interspersed
with quiet-water stretches. The stream, even today, teems
with trout. If anything, it contains too many fish. Small
brook trout, many undersized, abound in almost every
pool of the De Grasse headwaters. They are as bad a
nuisance as chubs and no angler with any conservation
ideas would want to fish in such water for long. You
simply can't avoid killing some of these oversized minnows
which apparently cannot grow up because there are too
many fish for the amount of natural food in the stream.
Downstream are fine stretches that contain many fair-sized
rainbows which I suspect, grow up partly on the meat of
the small brookies. As you work downstream, increasing
numbers of long, but lean, brown trout appear.

In case you may be thinking of fishing the De Grasse because of what you have read here, you'd better forget it. There isn't a good stretch on the stream, to my knowledge, that isn't tightly posted and patrolled by a series of well-managed fish and game clubs with highly-restricted memberships.

I've been fortunate to be able to fish this stream a number of times as the guest of Phil, one of the most enthusiastic trout anglers I know. Now in his late sixties, Phil's hands still shake every time he catches a fair trout, even though he might deny that hotly. If there are trout to be outwitted, Phil will keep going when many a younger man would be exhausted.

It was like that on the De Grasse one hot day early in June. We had caught piddling brookies by the dozens in the upper stretches of the river that morning. We came into the clubhouse for lunch. The caretaker, who also doubled as patrol officer and guide, told us of some big brown trout in a certain stretch downstream that "you can't catch at this time of the year; the only time you can get them is early in spring." He said there were few brookies or rainbows in that stretch.

There is nothing I like better than problem fish. Those are the type that no one can fail to catch without a glow of accomplishment. I could hardly wait until we finished our lunch. Another club member decided to accompany us.

The three of us fished for hours through the hot afternoon before we started to come to the conclusion that the caretaker was right. These brownies, if they existed, sure were tough. By five o'clock, we hadn't taken one fish big enough to keep. Between us, we used dry flies, wet flies, streamers, worms, and spinning lures. Phil used the latter, fishing them across-stream and permitting them to swing down.

I decided to try upstream spinning. I went back to the car for my gear and worked over to the other side of the river through a maze of slippery boulders to get to water none of us had fished. My second cast into a pocket under a tree-shaded boulder along the far bank produced an eighteen-inch brown. I lost an even larger fish in a deep run fifty feet upstream. Then, a few mintes later, I hooked and landed a skinny sixteen-incher. Within an hour, when we had to leave the stream for dinner at the clubhouse, I kept six trout, none under thirteen inches. It might be assumed that the trout had gone on the feed during that hour, but Phil and the other member, fishing in other ways, took only two small brownies.

I've fished that same stretch with success on a number of other occasions. If nothing else would work on it, either worms or spinning lures would. But there is no doubt that those trout were finicky. There was nothing half-way about them. It was a rare day when they would take flies. It was either worms or it was lures, quite decisively. If it was worms, they wouldn't take lures. If it was lures, they wouldn't take worms. Usually trout will go part way with you on these methods and you can catch some fish, whichever method you chose.

Before going further in discussing upstream spinning, we should emphasize one major reason why it is simpler and more effective for the relative newcomer to trout fishing.

The reason is that the long casts you are able to make with spinning gear minimize greatly the necessity of a careful stream approach. When you can easily cast seventy-five feet or more and don't have to worry about avoiding drag, or keeping out of a trout's "window," you escape most of the problems that confront an angler trying to work with a short line.

A good fly man and a few wormers can cast seventy-five feet too but they can't fish effectively at that distance on most water. The longer their line, generally, the more probability of drag.

In comparison with a fly man or wormer, the upstream spincaster can be almost careless in plowing along a stream, but, even here, some care is advisable. I've often suspected that Frank Cramer could do better with his slow retrieves if he'd walk a little more lightly. Frank actually pounds along a stream with little attempt to be quiet. He relies on a long line. Especially on a quiet stream, some of those vibrations are bound to carry to fish, even though they may be seventy-five feet away.

In upstream spinning, the ideal way to fish every pool is from the point where a riffle breaks out of it. Then you don't even have to worry about spooking fish that may be lying in the tail of the pool. The cast is made as directly upstream as possible. A lure coming directly downstream seems to be more attractive than one that has been cast quartering upstream. That is particularly true with the weighted spinners, which seem to simulate an insect more than a minnow. An insect floating downstream goes pretty much with the current. When you are using the minnow-type lure, the direct-upstream cast is less important.

It happens frequently that you cannot cast directly upstream because of obstructions such as an overhanging tree, a bend in the stream or a protruding log. But you still can bring that lure directly downstream by some rapid footwork and a shift in the position of the rod.

Buck is a master of the latter technique. Many times I've seen him cast with his rod in a vertical position, then quickly take a few steps to the side and hold his rod in a horizontal position so that he could bring a lure directly downstream close to some bush or overhanging bank.

Making shifts like this while starting an immediate re-trieve and keeping your reel handle revolving rapidly requires some co-ordination and practice, but it can be learned without too much effort. For some situations, it is highly productive.

When you are seventy-five feet away from a fish, there is less need to keep low. For this reason, it is quite practical to cast from low banks, reeling the lure close in to the edge of the bank. In this type of cast, of course, you should hold the rod tip as near the water and as near the bank as possible. Holding the tip near the water keeps the lure running deeper. If you hook a good fish from the bank, particularly if there are snags, you will have to try to get into the stream so that you can apply more effective lever-age to keep the trout away from the snags.

An important point about reeling should be emphasized strongly. It might seem insignificant but it makes a great deal of difference.

In Fred Turner's first days of upstream spinning, Buck and I couldn't figure out why he wasn't taking more fish. He cast well and in the right places, but the fish he took didn't compare with those Buck took or even with mine.

This went on for quite a few fishing expeditions before Buck noticed the sharp vibrations in Fred's rod as he was reeling in. With each decisive crank of the reel handle, Fred was transmitting down to the rod tip a similarly decisive tremor. Once the rod vibrations started, they be-came more pronounced as the reeling continued. The lure moved in jerks instead of smoothly. A smoothly moving lure always seems to be more effective.

After we explained to Fred what he was doing, he was able to correct the situation easily. As soon as he started to reel more smoothly the rhythmic rod vibrations became much less pronounced and Fred's batting average went up sharply. In fact, about fifteen minutes after he started to practice smoother reeling, he caught the largest fish of the day.

In discussing desirable reels for worming earlier, we mentioned our liking for the closed-spool fly rod type of reel. It should be stressed strongly right now that this type of reel is not the best for either worming or spinning. They are troublesome at times, but they are a good compromise solution to the problem: what kind of fishing are you going to do today?

When you leave your car to walk to a favored stretch of water, it isn't practical in most cases to carry both a long fly rod for worming and a spinning rod and open-spool spinning reel. If you are in doubt what type of equipment to string up, the fly rod and closed-spool spinning reel provide a good answer.

I've used a Johnson closed-spool reel for years, whenever I'm not sure whether worms or spinning lures will be most effective on a particular stream. I make a point of taking it whenever I fish quieter streams or streams with many quiet pools. It is on such streams that upstream spinning usually is deadliest.

With the closed-end spool and a fly rod it is a simple matter to shift from worms to lures. You can't cast as accurately at longer distances with the fly rod, but the greater length of the rod gives you enough additional leverage so that you can cast as far. With the long rod held in a horizontal position, you can often lead lures through snags or past hides more effectively than with the shorter rod. But the big advantage of this type of equipment is that, with a relatively short line, it permits placing of lures into snag-ridden and bush-covered pockets that no spin caster with conventional equipment would even attempt.

The accuracy is attained by fishing the lure with the same underhand cast used in worming, permitting line to shoot out from the reel through your fingers. In this type of lure casting, of course, we are right back to the same problems of careful stream approach that occur in worm-fishing but, on some stretches, such casting is extremely effective.

Fishing behind Buck with conventional spinning gear is a waste of time. He seems to move just about every trout that intends to be moved with a lure. But I was forced into it one day on the Wiscoy. We started in at the same point on a quiet stretch bordered with many thick tangles of alders. Buck started upstream. I planned to walk down-stream several hundred yards and then start upstream.

Buck was hardly out of sight around a bend in the stream, however, before I spotted no fewer than four anglers working toward me. It was a choice of fishing waters these four had pounded or water that Buck had covered. Buck fishes a stream quietly and I decided on the lesser of two evils. I could have used worms, but I decided on short-line spinning.

I didn't make a single cast into a hide I knew Buck must have fished. I concentrated entirely on the deep-in pockets way back in the alders. Sometimes my lure would move only a few feet before it stopped as my rod hit a branch. I snagged up often and lost more lures than I like to lose but I caught trout.

I knew that the long line Buck was casting forced him to bring it past the outside edge of these alders. He couldn't go in as deep as I could with the short line and fly rod. As I worked upstream after Buck, I didn't even consider a cast unless I could get several feet inside of Buck's limit. You never catch up with Buck. He's a racehorse on a stream. When I met him coming downstream, we compared catches. My catch was as good as his.

I've mentioned several times that upstream spinning is particularly effective on quiet stretches. For my money, it is the only consistently effective method on those still-water pools that you know contain good fish that will not take a fly or even a worm. On such pools, even though your fly or worm is not taken by the chubs that seem to abound, neither the fly or worm get much, if any, stream action. Often they will lie lifelessly in one spot until you shift their position. With a spinning lure, you are in business on such pools.

For obvious reasons, I will not give the exact location of one particular pool of that type on a Western New York stream that, season after season, has yielded dozens of pounds of trout to our spinning rods. The supply of fish seems limitless; yet I've succeeded in taking only a few fish from this pool with a fly or worm.

The unglamorous pool is within a village. Downstream from it is a bridge. Nearby is a combination restaurant and tavern. It is the kind of pool that an angler who wants beauty would never fish. It is long and sluggish with virtually no current at its tail. You can wade across almost any part of it in rubber boots. The hides consist of a few, scrawny bushes hanging into the water and several overhanging trees.

Buck and I first fished this pool on a boiling-hot day in August when our success had been only fair. The fish we had taken had been creeled early in the morning. We stopped in at the tavern to quench our thirst.

When we came out, we looked over the stream bank before getting into the car. The water was shallow and unpromising. Then Buck spotted two good fish lying in the shade of the bank on the far side of the stream. He dashed to the car for his spinning rod. I was content to sit on the bank and watch.

Buck went to the downstream side of the bridge before he entered the stream. He worked up in the shallows under the bridge before casting. As usual, his cast was right on the button, about ten feet upstream from where the trout were lying. I could clearly see one of the trout intercept the weighted spinner. Soon after, he landed a fifteen-inch brown.

The other trout had disappeared but Buck started to work up through the pool, making longer-than-usual casts. Before he reached the head of the pool, where a gentle riffle flowed into it, he had taken three more trout. One was seventeen inches, the smallest thirteen inches.

We've fished that pool dozens of times since. It's a kind of ace-in-the-hole, where we can take fish almost every time we try it, even though trout may be having an off day on other stretches of the same stream.

Downstream from the pool, the water in the stream is livelier. In that stretch, I don't remember a day in which worms didn't decisively outfish a spinning lure, but when we came to that quiet pool, it was lures or nothing.

There's another still-water pool near the headwaters of Elton Creek which we've found is almost exclusively a pool for lures. I had sneaked up to the edge of a riffle leading into this pool one day. At the time I was on my rump only inches from the water. I was trying to float a worm into the pool on a slack line when a big trout, which I may have frightened, scurried up into the riffle, part of its back out of water, and actually splashed water into my face. I kept my eyes on the fish and saw it drop back into the quiet part of the pool, then swing under an overhanging bush in about two feet of glassy water. Very carefully, I withdrew from my position at the side of the riffle, made a new approach so that I could reach the big fish and waited as long as I could stand it before casting. I hooked a chub almost immediately. That ended that. I tried for that fish twice more with worms on subsequent days without success.

I told Buck about it one day in which I had taken several good fish on worms farther downstream. Buck hadn't taken a fish with lures. I led him to the pool. He cast so his lure would pass close to that bush, which I figured was the trout's hangout. The fish took his weighted spinner explosively, thrashing violently as it felt the hook. It was a long, nip-and-tuck battle marked by irresistible runs all over the pool and much thrashing. Then the trout started downstream through another riffle into a snag-ridden pool. If the trout had ever made that pool, Buck probably would have lost it.

His four-pound test line never would have withstood all those logs and sunken brush. He couldn't stop the fish, but, just before it reached the snaggy pool, Buck let up on the pressure and the trout turned upstream again. He netted it soon after. It weighed four and one-half pounds.

Phil Savage convinced himself of the effectiveness of spinning lures one day on the DeGrasse River in which, up to that time, he had taken only a few trout that were worth keeping. He had been using flies and worms. He's a good fly man but hasn't learned all the technique of worm fishing. Anyway, neither produced much for him on a certain large pool below a shelving cascade that was half-way between a waterfall and a rapids. The pool is so large and so deep that it is virtually impossible to fish all of it with casts made directly upstream, but Phil did the best anyone could do after switching to a lure. He used a wobbling spoon and cast to the far side of the pool, near the cascade, so that the rushing water would belly his line and drag the lure downstream. This is good technique in such a situation and it paid off well for him. On that day and on subsequent days, Phil hooked and landed enough heavy fish to make him a strong convert to the use of lures under certain conditions.

On one of those late-August days after several cool nights, Fred Turner and I had a convincing demonstration of the effectiveness of lures after we had used worms for several hours. We were fishing a quiet stretch of Ischua Creek, in which we knew there were many good fish. The water was very low and we soon realized that even the most careful approach wasn't good enough. We walked back to the car and strung up conventional spinning gear. Within two hours we kept four fish weighing a total of eight and one-half pounds and released five more that, on another day, we'd have been glad to keep.

Why trout in quiet pools sometimes are not frightened by the splash of the lures or the knifing of the line through the water I cannot say. At those times, I suspect that the lure attracts their attention to the exclusion of all else. Possibly leaping chubs have made them accustomed to splashes. In this connection, you can minimize the splash of the lure, if it must be cast into quiet water, by making low bullet casts to a point several feet above your target or sidearm casts. When you stop the lure before it enters the water, it will fall with less commotion. A high, arching cast in this type of situation will mean much more commotion. Also, a high cast usually means more difficulty in taking slack out of your line and starting the retrieve immediately.

chapter 20

Broil-Smoking Trout

LIKE SO MANY ARDENT TROUT ANGLERS, I NEVER WAS
particularly fond of eating fish I had caught. Oh, I
wouldn't mind them once in a while but there are so
many of my trout-loving friends on an eager waiting list
that, one by one, I usually have preferred to take care of
them.

Several years ago, a native Californian changed my mind
about eating trout. Give me conditions for preparing them
in the way he prepared them and, brother, try to keep
me away.

I got my easy lesson in cookery at the Old Faithful
campsite in Yellowstone Park, where my wife and I had
parked our little house trailer. For more than a week, I
fished there with Brady Palla and Pappy Philbrick of
Paso Robles. We all did well on the Firehole, Madison,
and Lewis Rivers but I gave most of the few fish I kept
to Brady and Pappy.

I ate trout once and quit. As yet, I hadn't seen how
those fellows cooked their trout.

Then, on the day before Brady and Pappy had to leave for home, a No. 14 Light Cahill produced some magnificent fish for me on the stillwater stretch of the Lewis River. There was a gorgeous five-and-a-half-pound Loch Leven and several other fine fish. Brady wanted a few good fish to take home and he now had them. He was glad but anxious to convert me into an enthusiastic trout eater. So, we put aside several medium-sized fish and Brady came over to our campsite that evening to prepare them.

I wasn't impressed at first. It appeared that I was going to get only the ordinary broiled trout to which I had become accustomed. Brady started a small fire in an outdoor fireplace and placed the trout in a handle-type wire grill.

He waited for the fire, small as it was, to die down before placing the grill on the pipe platform in the fireplace. I started to kid him about his fire. There wasn't enough heat to cause the trout to sizzle until they had been over the fire for ten minutes or more. Brady ignored me.

On the way back to camp, we had stopped to collect a few live limbs, about an inch in diameter, from some scrubby aspen trees, often called "popple" trees. Brady added pieces of these greenish-colored limbs to the fire. They smouldered. The smoke was delightfully sweet and spicy, more appealing even than the smoke from hickory or apple wood.

Brady flipped the grill every few minutes. There was almost as much smoke as heat. He permitted no flame. If any appeared, he moved the smouldering wood around until the flame stopped. If the fire became too hot, he removed some of the embers. As soon as the trout would barely start to sizzle, he'd turn the grill.

After about a half-hour, I wanted to know when the heck we were going to eat but Brady looked at me scornfully and continued to nurse the fire, flip the grill, and move out of the way of the smoke. The fire was so low that it must have required forty-five minutes before those trout started to become brown. At approximately the one-hour mark, the brownness started to become delectable. Little droplets of oil from the fish appeared to be basting that luscious brownness into a tender crisp. My wife's eyes started to get that eager look, the kind of look they get when we pass the window of a good bakery while wonderful baking smells come out of an open door. My mouth started to water. I'd never seen trout like this before.

It was nearly one-and-a-half hours before Brady rose from his crouched position and brought the trout triumphantly over to our camp table.

Never since have I been anything but eager to eat trout prepared in this way. They were wonderfully juicy, but some of that typical, decisive trout flavor was gone. Instead, there was something new added—the sweet spice of the aspen smoke, delicate but unmistakable. My wife and I ate every scrap with relish. We've eaten many such scraps since.

chapter 21

Worming or Spinning?

DECIDING WHETHER TO BECOME A GOOD WORMER OR AN upstream spincaster depends on the individual. The more you know about all phases of trout fishing—or about anything else, for that matter—the better for you. The best solution in this case is to learn both.

On the average, worming will enable you to take the greatest poundage of brown trout with the most consistency on the average Eastern stream. But applying all the techniques of worming at the same time is far more difficult than doing a first-class job of spinning.

As pointed out previously, successful worming requires more than proper tackle, small worms, a good stream or a fine day. It means more than good technique, more than stream knowledge, more than a skillful approach to a trout's suspected hiding place. It means a fine combination of all of these things at the same time. Forget or ignore any of the important factors and your success will dwindle proportionately.

If you come to the conclusion that you can't apply

154

yourself diligently enough to become a good wormer, the chances are that you would be better off using your time on a stream with a spinning rod. You can make glaring mistakes with the latter and still take many nice fish. You can't make glaring mistakes in worming and do well. In worming, you must go all the way, with everything you know—all at the same time. Become careless in any phase of worming, even though you may be doing everything else right, and the results will show it. You can't be almost automatic, or fish mostly on instinct with worms, even though it is possible with spinning lures. With worms, you concentrate or else. That's what makes it so interesting, so challenging.

Again, on the average, it might be said safely that you will take larger fish with properly fished lures than you will with worms. This is no contradiction of the statement made earlier in this chapter that you will take a greater poundage of brown trout with worms. With lures, you will take an occasional whopper, more whoppers than with worms.

But, day in and day out, you will take more brownies in the twelve- to eighteen-inch class with properly fished worms. In the case of larger rainbows and brookies, not piddlers, I think lures will hold their own in comparison with worms.

When you use a lure, you don't have to fuss around digging and scouring worms. You don't even have to get your hands dirty handling them.

On the other hand, you will get far less fight from a lure-hooked trout, generally, than you will get from a trout hooked with a worm, even a trout hooked deeply with a worm. Somehow, those treble hooks used on most lures seem to cause a trout to flounder almost helplessly when you play it toward you. Unless it's a large fish, a lure-hooked trout will do far less jumping, make far fewer rushes on the average. They'll thrash but they seem far less able to cope with the lures.

These latter statements apply even though you may be using a spinning rod as dainty as a light fly rod. The relative lack of fight in fish hooked is my principal gripe against spinning. Maybe there's an answer, but none of our boys has been able to figure it out.

Sometimes two of us have worked a stream together, the spinning man slightly ahead. It happens often that trout will rise to a lure but not take. The spinner will notify the wormer of the location of the fish. The wormer will move in and, often, with the knowledge of the almost exact location, will take it. Such teamwork can be deadly if the spinner guards against exposing himself to fish that the wormer hopes to lure.

Even a thorough knowledge of the techniques of worming and spinning will not be enough in themselves to enable you to take trout consistently. You'll have to practice accuracy, to apply on the streams the methods you've learned. Apply well the techniques you've learned here and you'll seldom be "skunked" again on your favorite trout stream.